BEYOND THE MIND
ENDING SUFFERING
THROUGH INNER PEACE

NANCY B BLEVINS

Published by Nancy B. Blevins
733 CACTUS LN
SAN ANGELO
TX,76903
All inquiries should be addressed to the publisher.
First Edition: 2024
ISBN: 9798340293527
Printed in the United States of America
The author acknowledges the rights of the original owners of the quotes, teachings,
and ideas referenced in this book, which are attributed to their respective sources.

DEDICATION

To all those seeking peace beyond the noise of the mind,
may you find the stillness within yourself.
To my family and friends, for your unwavering love and support,
and to every reader who embarks on this journey,
may you discover the inner freedom that has always been yours.
This book is for you.

TABLE OF CONTENTS

ACKNOWLEDGMENTS

This book would not have been possible without the guidance, support, and inspiration of so many individuals along the way. First and foremost, I would like to express my deepest gratitude to my family, whose love and encouragement have been a constant source of strength and motivation throughout this journey. Your belief in me has kept me grounded and inspired, and for that, I am eternally grateful.

To my close friends and colleagues, thank you for your wisdom, feedback, and thoughtful conversations that have helped shape the ideas in this book. Your insights have been invaluable, and I deeply appreciate your honesty and support throughout the writing process.

A special thanks to the many teachers, both past and present, whose wisdom has influenced my understanding of mindfulness, Zen, and non-thinking. Your teachings have not only shaped the content of this book but have also transformed my own life in profound ways.

I would also like to thank my editor, whose keen eye and thoughtful suggestions helped bring clarity and coherence to my work. Your dedication to the craft and your attention to detail have been crucial in bringing this book to life.

To all the readers and students who have shared their experiences and journeys with me, thank you. Your stories and reflections have been a source of inspiration and have reminded me why this work is so important. It is through your courage and willingness to explore the depths of the mind that the lessons in this book come to life.

Finally, to every person who has ever struggled with the mind's endless chatter, anxiety, or overthinking—this book is for you. May it serve as a guide and a reminder that peace is always within reach, beyond the mind.

INTRODUCTION

UNLOCK THE POWER OF PRESENCE HOW TO NAVIGATE THIS BOOK FOR TRANSFORMATION

Welcome, dear reader, to the journey of transformation that awaits you within these pages. This book is not just another self-help guide to tell you how to live, but rather a profound exploration of your mind, your thoughts, and how you can finally unlock the peace that has always existed within you. You are not here by accident. Something in your life has likely brought you to this point—a yearning for change, a desire to find deeper meaning, or perhaps an inner struggle that refuses to settle. Whatever the case, this book is your companion, not your teacher, as we explore together the power of presence and how to free yourself from the mental traps that cause suffering.

Before we dive into the chapters that await, let's take a moment to understand how you can use this book to guide you, challenge you, and most importantly, transform you. Transformation is not something that comes from simply reading a text—it is an experience, a practice, and a way of being. Therefore, my invitation to you is to see this book as more than words on a page. Consider it a mirror through which you will begin to see yourself and the world around you differently.

The Nature of Thought and the Journey Ahead

Many of us live in a constant state of mental activity, our minds filled with an endless stream of thoughts. These thoughts range from the mundane tasks of everyday life to deep concerns about our future, our identity, and our purpose. And while thinking is often seen as a sign of intelligence, innovation, and human progress, it can also be the very root of our suffering.

You may wonder, how can thinking—the thing that defines our human experience—be the source of pain? The answer is not so much in the thinking itself but in our relationship with thought. Most of us are never taught how to separate ourselves from the thoughts we think. We identify with them, believe them, and let them shape our emotions, behaviors, and lives. But here's the secret that many ancient spiritual traditions have known for centuries: **you are not your thoughts.**

This concept may sound simple or even obvious, but living it is far from easy. It is the very core of your transformation. Once you learn to observe your thoughts rather than be controlled by them, you open up the vast expanse of presence—the true state of being that is free from mental suffering. And it is in this space, beyond the noise of constant thinking, that you can finally experience peace, joy, and true fulfillment.

How to Use This Book

You are about to embark on a journey that will challenge your current understanding of yourself, your mind, and your life. The chapters that follow are designed to guide you through the process of untangling the web of thought and finding freedom from the suffering that thinking creates. Here's how you can make the most out of your experience with this book:

Read Slowly, Reflect Deeply – This is not a book to rush through. Each chapter contains concepts and practices that will likely stir something deep within you. Take your time with each section. Reflect on how the ideas apply to your own life. Don't be afraid to put the book down after a particularly resonant paragraph and simply sit with it.

Practice Presence as You Read – Presence is not something you achieve at the end of this book. It's something you can begin cultivating from the very first page. As you read, practice being fully present with the words and ideas. Notice any distractions that arise and gently bring your attention back to the moment. This will not only enhance your understanding but will also be a powerful exercise in mindful awareness.

Apply the Concepts to Your Life – The true power of this book comes from applying what you learn. After each chapter, take some time to integrate the teachings into your daily life. Whether it's observing your thoughts, practicing non-thinking, or finding moments of stillness throughout your day, these practices will help you embody the transformation that this book offers.

Be Patient with Yourself – Transformation does not happen overnight. You may find some chapters challenging, others enlightening, and still others confusing. That is perfectly okay. Be patient with yourself throughout this process. Change takes time, and there will be moments when your mind resists what it is learning. In those moments, remember to come back to presence.

Stay Open – Some of the ideas in this book may be unfamiliar or even uncomfortable at first. You may question them or feel resistant to their implications. I encourage you to stay open to new perspectives. It is through openness that true growth occurs. Let this book challenge your existing beliefs and assumptions, and you will find yourself expanding in ways you never imagined.

CHAPTER 1

THE HIDDEN PATH: UNRAVELING THE TRUE SOURCE OF SUFFERING

The Invisible Burden

Every human being, regardless of their external circumstances, is burdened with some form of suffering. Some carry it silently, while others wear it visibly on their sleeves. But whether acknowledged or hidden beneath the surface, suffering permeates the human experience. We seek answers, solutions, and ways to alleviate this burden, but often, these attempts at relief only provide temporary solace. The reason for this is that we are addressing suffering at the surface level, focusing on external circumstances—relationships, finances, career, health—without ever questioning its true origin.

In this chapter, we will embark on a journey to explore the hidden path that leads us to suffering. By the end of this chapter, you will have uncovered a deeper understanding of suffering's root cause and will be equipped with the knowledge to begin unraveling it, layer by layer. This exploration may challenge many of your current beliefs, but it will also open the door to a freedom you may have never thought possible.

The Common Misconception: Blaming the Outside World

We are conditioned, from an early age, to believe that the source of our suffering lies in the outside world. When something goes wrong in our lives, we instinctively look for external reasons to explain our distress. If we feel hurt, we assume it's because someone treated us poorly. If we feel anxious, we blame our job, our financial situation, or the uncertainty of the future. If we feel grief, we attribute it to the loss of a loved one. In all of these instances, our immediate reaction is to point to something or someone outside of ourselves as the cause of our suffering.

This perspective is not without merit. Of course, external circumstances can trigger emotional pain. Life is full of unpredictable events, and it's natural to experience grief, disappointment, frustration, and anxiety in response to the challenges we face. But what if the external events themselves are not the true source of our suffering? What if they are merely the catalysts that reveal an underlying, internal process that is the real cause of our pain?

Imagine for a moment that you are wearing a pair of sunglasses with a dark tint. As you go about your day, the world around you appears dim and shadowed. It would be easy to conclude that the world itself is dark and lacking in light. But if you remove the sunglasses, you would see that the world has not changed—it was only your perception of it that was altered. In the same way, our suffering is often a result of the "tint" through which we view the world— our thoughts, beliefs, and mental patterns. When we learn to shift our perception, we begin to see that suffering is not a fixed, external reality but something that arises from within.

The Role of Thought in Creating Suffering

The first key to understanding the true source of suffering lies in recognizing the role that thought plays in shaping our experience. The human mind is an extraordinary tool—it allows us to analyze, create, imagine, and solve problems. But it also has a darker side: it has the capacity to generate endless streams of negative, self-defeating, and fearful thoughts. And it is these thoughts that often give rise to suffering.

When we experience a painful event, our minds quickly go to work, generating thoughts that amplify and sustain the emotional pain. For example, imagine you lose your job. While the initial event may trigger feelings of shock or disappointment, it is the thoughts that follow—"I'm a failure," "I'll never find another job," "What will people think of me?"—that create a deeper layer of suffering. These thoughts, unchecked, can spiral into anxiety, depression, and even despair.

The same pattern occurs in almost every situation where we experience suffering. A breakup might lead to thoughts of unworthiness or fear of being alone. A health scare might lead to thoughts of hopelessness or fear of death. In each case, the mind takes the initial event and magnifies it through the lens of thought, turning what could be a momentary discomfort into prolonged suffering.

But here's the important distinction: while the event may be out of our control, the thoughts that follow are not. We cannot always change what happens to us, but we can learn to change how we respond to it mentally. By becoming aware of the thoughts that arise in response to pain, we can begin to disentangle ourselves from the mental narratives that perpetuate suffering.

The Cycle of Identification with Thought

Why do we suffer so deeply from our thoughts? The answer lies in a phenomenon known as identification with thought. Most of us are so deeply identified with our thoughts that we believe them to be an inherent part of who we are. When a negative thought arises—such as "I am not good enough"—we don't see it as a temporary mental construct; we see it as a reflection of our true self.

This identification with thought is what gives thoughts their power. If you believe that your thoughts are an accurate reflection of reality, you will suffer every time a painful or fearful thought arises. On the other hand, if you can learn to see your thoughts as just that—thoughts, not reality—you begin to loosen the grip they have on you.

Consider the example of someone who struggles with social anxiety. Every time they enter a social situation, their mind generates thoughts like "I'm going to embarrass myself" or "People are judging me." If they are identified with these thoughts, they will experience intense anxiety and discomfort, believing that these thoughts are accurate reflections of reality. But if they can learn to observe these thoughts without identifying with them—recognizing them as fleeting mental constructs rather than truth—they can begin to reduce their suffering and experience more peace in social situations.

The key to breaking the cycle of identification with thought is mindfulness. Mindfulness allows us to observe our thoughts without becoming entangled in them. When we practice mindfulness, we create a space between ourselves and our thoughts, allowing us to see them for what they are: temporary, impermanent mental events. In that space, we find freedom from the tyranny of thought.

The Illusion of Control

Another significant contributor to human suffering is the illusion of control. We often believe that if we can just control our circumstances—if we can make everything in our external world perfect—then we will be happy and free from suffering. This belief leads to a constant striving for control, as we attempt to manipulate our environment, relationships, and experiences to match our desires.

But the truth is, control is an illusion. No matter how hard we try, we cannot control everything in our lives. The world is inherently unpredictable, and things will not always go according to plan. This realization can be deeply unsettling for many people, as it confronts us with the reality of our own vulnerability and powerlessness.

The more we cling to the illusion of control, the more we suffer. When we believe that we must control everything in order to be happy, we set ourselves up for disappointment and frustration, because life will inevitably throw us curveballs. We may get laid off from a job, experience the end of a relationship, or face a health crisis—none of which we can fully control. And when these events occur, the belief that we should have been able to control them only adds to our suffering.

The antidote to this illusion is surrender. Surrender does not mean giving up or becoming passive; rather, it means accepting the reality that we cannot control everything and finding peace in that acceptance. When we stop resisting the flow of life and start embracing the present moment as it is, we open ourselves to a deeper sense of peace and freedom.

The Role of the Ego in Sustaining Suffering

At the heart of much of our suffering is the ego. The ego is the part of us that is constantly seeking to define itself, protect itself, and assert its importance. It is the voice in our heads that says, "I am right, they are wrong," "I need to be successful to be worthy," "I must be liked by others to be happy." The ego thrives on comparison, judgment, and a sense of separateness from others.

The ego is also deeply invested in suffering, because suffering reinforces its sense of identity. When we suffer, we often feel a heightened sense of self—"I am the one who is hurt," "I am the one who has been wronged." This sense of self is comforting to the ego, even if the suffering itself is painful. In this way, the ego has a vested interest in keeping us stuck in cycles of suffering, because it reinforces the illusion of separateness and strengthens the ego's sense of importance.

The more we identify with the ego, the more we suffer. The ego is never satisfied—it always wants more, whether it's more success, more approval, or more control. And when it doesn't get what it wants, it reacts with anger, frustration, and disappointment. In this way, the ego keeps us trapped in a perpetual state of dissatisfaction and suffering.

The key to transcending the ego is awareness. When we become aware of the ego's patterns and tendencies, we can begin to disidentify from it. We can see the ego for what it is—a collection of thoughts, beliefs, and desires—and recognize that it is not the true essence of who we are. By cultivating this awareness, we can begin to loosen the ego's grip on us and experience a deeper sense of peace and freedom.

Embracing Impermanence

One of the most profound truths that can help us unravel the source of suffering is the recognition of impermanence. Everything in life is impermanent—our thoughts, our emotions, our experiences, our relationships, and even our physical bodies. Yet, we often live as though things are permanent, clinging to the belief that we can hold on to the things we love and avoid the things we fear.

This clinging to permanence is a major source of suffering. When we try to hold on to something that is inherently impermanent, we set ourselves up for disappointment and pain. For example, when we cling to a relationship, believing that it will never change, we are devastated when the relationship ends or evolves in ways we didn't expect. Similarly, when we cling to youth, beauty, or health, we suffer when the natural process of aging or illness occurs.

The solution to this suffering is not to avoid attachment or to suppress our desires, but to embrace the reality of impermanence. When we learn to accept that everything in life is constantly changing, we can begin to let go of our need to control and hold on to things. This doesn't mean we stop caring or stop striving for meaningful experiences, but it means we approach life with a sense of openness and non-attachment.

By embracing impermanence, we can experience life more fully. Instead of resisting change, we learn to flow with it. Instead of clinging to the past or fearing the future, we can live in the present moment with a sense of gratitude and acceptance. This shift in perspective allows us to experience life with more joy, peace, and freedom.

The Power of Presence in Dissolving Suffering

The culmination of this exploration of suffering leads us to the practice of presence. Presence is the state of being fully aware and engaged in the present moment, free from the distractions of thought, judgment, and ego. When we are present, we are not identified with our thoughts or caught up in the stories that our minds create. We are simply aware of what is happening, without resistance or attachment.

Presence is the antidote to suffering because it allows us to experience life as it truly is, rather than through the distorted lens of thought. When we are present, we are not worried about the future or ruminating on the past. We are not caught up in the drama of the ego or the illusions of control. Instead, we are fully here, in the now, where peace and freedom reside.

The practice of presence is simple, but not always easy. It requires us to cultivate awareness of our thoughts, emotions, and surroundings, and to gently bring our attention back to the present moment whenever we notice our minds wandering. Over time, with consistent practice, presence becomes our natural state of being, and suffering begins to dissolve.

The Hidden Path Revealed

In this chapter, we have explored the hidden path that leads to suffering—a path that is not found in external circumstances, but within our own minds. We have uncovered the role of thought, the illusion of control, the ego's investment in suffering, and the power of impermanence. Most importantly, we have discovered that the key to dissolving suffering lies in the practice of presence.

As we move forward in this book, we will continue to deepen our understanding of these concepts and explore practical ways to apply them in our daily lives. The journey of transformation is not a quick fix, but a lifelong practice of awareness, presence, and acceptance. By walking this path, we can begin to unravel the true source of our suffering and experience the peace, joy, and freedom that have always been available to us.

CHAPTER 2

SUFFERING UNVEILED
DISCOVER THE ROOT CAUS

The Mask of Suffering

It is often said that suffering wears many masks, and no one is immune to its presence. We see it in the faces of those we pass by in the street, in the conversations we have with our loved ones, and even in the silent moments of our own solitude. It may appear as sorrow, fear, anger, frustration, or even a subtle undercurrent of dissatisfaction with life. Yet, beneath all these forms lies a singular root cause, a source that remains hidden from plain sight.

In this chapter, we will journey further down the path we began in Chapter 1, peeling back the layers of suffering to reveal its true origin. We will explore the subtle workings of the mind and ego, as well as the false narratives that keep us trapped in cycles of pain. Through the teachings of Zen masters and other spiritual traditions, we will uncover the wisdom that has been passed down through generations, offering us insight into the timeless truth of suffering's root cause.

The Zen Perspective: Suffering is Not in the World, It is in the Mind

Zen teachings often focus on the mind as both the source of suffering and the key to liberation. As Zen Master Thich Nhat Hanh says,

"People have a hard time letting go of their suffering.
Out of a fear of the unknown, they prefer suffering that
is familiar."

This quote speaks to a fundamental truth: suffering is not inherent in the world itself but is a product of the mind's attachment to certain ideas, beliefs, and perceptions.

10

The world, in its pure form, is neutral. It is neither good nor bad, neither pleasant nor unpleasant. It is our interpretation of the world—our thoughts, judgments, and desires—that give rise to suffering. Zen Buddhism teaches us that the root of suffering lies in the mind's tendency to cling to things as they are or as we believe they should be. Whether it is a desire for something we do not have, an attachment to something we fear losing, or a resistance to what is happening in the present moment, the mind creates suffering by trying to control or resist reality.

This understanding is critical because it shifts the focus of our suffering from external circumstances to our own mental processes. If suffering were caused by the world itself, we would be powerless to change it. But if suffering is a product of the mind, then we have the power to transform it by changing how we relate to our thoughts, feelings, and experiences.

The Role of Desire and Attachment

At the heart of Zen teachings is the concept of attachment as the primary cause of suffering. The Buddha's Four Noble Truths, the foundation of all Buddhist teachings, state that life is suffering (dukkha), and the cause of suffering is attachment (tanha). Whether we are attached to material possessions, relationships, or even our own self-image, this clinging creates a constant state of tension and dissatisfaction.

Consider this example: You may have a deep attachment to your career. You derive your sense of self-worth from your job title, your accomplishments, and the approval of your colleagues. But what happens when you experience a setback—when a project fails or when you are passed over for a promotion? If your sense of identity and value is tied to your career, this perceived failure becomes a personal failure. You suffer not because the event itself is inherently painful but because your attachment to a particular outcome creates the conditions for suffering.

Zen Master Shunryu Suzuki expressed this idea succinctly when he said,

"The most important point is to accept yourself and stand on your two feet."

When we attach our sense of self to external factors—our job, our relationships, our appearance—we become vulnerable to suffering because these things are impermanent and subject to change. But when we learn to accept ourselves as we are, without attachment to external validation, we free

11

ourselves from the constant cycle of suffering.

The Ego's Role in Perpetuating Suffering

Closely related to attachment is the role of the ego in sustaining suffering. The ego is the aspect of the mind that seeks to create and maintain a sense of individual identity. It is concerned with defining "who I am" and "who I am not," and it operates through a lens of comparison, judgment, and separateness.

The ego is deeply invested in the stories we tell ourselves about our lives. It clings to identities such as "the successful professional," "the caring parent," "the victim of circumstance," or "the strong, independent person." These identities give the ego a sense of stability and importance, but they also create suffering when reality doesn't align with the ego's expectations.

For example, if you identify strongly with the role of "the successful professional," any setback in your career feels like a threat to your very identity. The ego cannot tolerate the idea of failure, so it reacts with feelings of fear, anxiety, or frustration. This emotional response is not a result of the situation itself but of the ego's attachment to a particular self-image.

As Zen Master Dogen once said,

> *"To study the self is to forget the self. To forget the self is to be enlightened by all things."*

This quote speaks to the Zen understanding that true freedom comes from letting go of the ego's attachments and dissolving the sense of separateness that keeps us bound to suffering. When we "forget the self"—meaning, when we stop identifying so strongly with our thoughts, roles, and identities—we open ourselves to a greater sense of connection with the world and a deeper experience of peace.

The Illusion of Control and Its Relationship to Suffering

Another key cause of suffering is the illusion of control. Many of us operate under the belief that if we can just control our external circumstances, we can avoid suffering and be happy. We strive to control our careers, our relationships, our health, and even the behavior of others, believing that this will lead to security and satisfaction. But in reality, the more we try to control, the more we suffer.

Zen teaches that control is an illusion because life is inherently unpredictable and impermanent. No matter how hard we try, we cannot control everything that happens to us. We cannot control the actions of others, the passing of time, or the natural ebb and flow of life's challenges. When we resist this reality, we create tension and suffering within ourselves.

As Zen Master Suzuki Roshi reminds us, "Life is like stepping onto a boat which is about to sail out to sea and sink." This quote is not meant to be pessimistic but rather a reflection of the impermanence of all things. Once we accept that life is constantly changing and that we cannot control its course, we can begin to let go of our futile attempts at control and find peace in the present moment.

The Mind's Stories: How We Create Suffering Through Interpretation

The mind has an incredible capacity to create stories about the events in our lives. These stories often take the form of judgments, interpretations, and projections about what is happening and what it means for us. While the events themselves are neutral, it is the stories we tell about them that create suffering.

For example, imagine you receive critical feedback from your boss. The event itself is neutral—it is simply information about how your performance is being perceived. But the mind quickly creates a story: "My boss doesn't like me," "I'm not good enough," "I'm going to lose my job." These thoughts trigger a cascade of emotions—fear, anxiety, self-doubt—and before you know it, you are suffering not because of the feedback itself but because of the story you have created around it.

In Zen, this process of creating stories is often referred to as "mind-made suffering." The mind takes a simple event and adds layers of interpretation, judgment, and meaning that are not inherently present in the event itself. By learning to observe the mind's stories without becoming attached to them, we can begin to see reality more clearly and reduce the suffering that comes from these mental narratives.

Zen Master Thich Nhat Hanh offers a simple but powerful teaching:

"When you understand that everything is the way it is because of causes and conditions, you are able to let go of suffering."

This quote reminds us that everything we experience is the result of countless causes and conditions that are often beyond our control. By accepting this reality, we can let go of the mind's stories and find peace in the present moment.

The Role of Fear in Sustaining Suffering

Fear is one of the most powerful emotions that perpetuates suffering. Fear arises when we perceive a threat to our well-being, whether that threat is real or imagined. The mind's job is to protect us from danger, and it often does so by creating worst-case scenarios and worrying about the future. While this can be helpful in certain situations, it often leads to unnecessary suffering when fear becomes our default state of mind.

Zen teaches that much of our fear is based on illusion. We fear losing control, losing loved ones, losing our status or possessions, or even losing our sense of self. But these fears are often based on the ego's attachment to things that are impermanent. When we cling to things that are subject to change, we create fear because we know, deep down, that we cannot truly hold on to them.

As Zen Master Linji Yixuan wisely said,

"If you meet the Buddha, kill him."

This cryptic statement means that even our most cherished beliefs and attachments—including our spiritual beliefs—can become obstacles if we cling to them too tightly. In the same way, our fears are often illusions created by the mind's attachment to certain outcomes. By "killing" these illusions, we can free ourselves from fear and live more fully in the present moment.

Mindfulness: The Path to Freedom from Suffering

At the heart of Zen practice is mindfulness—the art of being fully present in each moment without judgment or attachment. Mindfulness allows us to see the root cause of our suffering more clearly, because it brings our attention to the thoughts, emotions, and patterns of behavior that perpetuate pain.

When we practice mindfulness, we create a space between ourselves and our thoughts. We learn to observe our thoughts without becoming entangled in them, and we begin to see that our suffering is not caused by external circumstances but by our reactions to those circumstances. As we cultivate mindfulness, we become more aware of the ways in which we create suffering for ourselves, and we develop the ability to choose more skillful responses to life's challenges.

Zen Master Thich Nhat Hanh explains,

> *"Mindfulness is like a lamp illuminating reality. The lamp is yourself, lit by the flame of your concentration. If your concentration is steady, you will see the root of your suffering."*

This quote highlights the power of mindfulness to reveal the root cause of suffering. When we shine the light of awareness on our thoughts, feelings, and behaviors, we can begin to dismantle the patterns that keep us trapped in suffering.

The Freedom of Non-Attachment

The ultimate goal of Zen practice is to cultivate a state of non-attachment—freedom from the clinging, craving, and aversion that create suffering. Non-attachment does not mean indifference or passivity; rather, it is a way of engaging with life fully and wholeheartedly while letting go of the need to control or possess.

When we practice non-attachment, we can enjoy life's pleasures without becoming enslaved by them. We can experience pain without becoming overwhelmed by it. We can navigate challenges with grace and equanimity, knowing that everything is impermanent and that our true nature is not defined by external circumstances.

As Zen Master Huang Po taught,

> *"The foolish reject what they see, not what they think; the wise reject what they think, not what they see."*

This quote speaks to the wisdom of letting go of our mental attachments and embracing the reality of each moment as it is. When we free ourselves from the mind's attachments, we discover a deeper, more lasting sense of peace and joy.

Unveiling the Root Cause of Suffering

In this chapter, we have uncovered the root cause of suffering: the mind's attachment to desires, outcomes, and identities. We have explored the role of the ego, the illusion of control, and the stories the mind creates to sustain suffering. Through the wisdom of Zen masters and the practice of mindfulness, we have seen that the path to freedom lies in letting go of attachment and embracing the present moment with openness and awareness.

As we continue on this journey, we will deepen our understanding of these concepts and explore practical ways to apply them in our daily lives. The root cause of suffering may be hidden, but with awareness, mindfulness, and a commitment to practice, we can unveil it and begin to experience the freedom that lies beyond.

CHAPTER 3

THE THINKING TRAP
WHY OUR MINDS SPIN

The Endless Stream of Thought

Every human being knows the feeling: the constant, restless activity of the mind that never seems to stop. Even when we try to relax or sleep, our thoughts continue to whirl, jumping from one idea to the next, often in a frenzy. This mental chatter can feel like a trap—an inescapable cycle of overthinking, analyzing, and worrying. Many of us feel powerless to stop it, resigned to the idea that a spinning mind is simply a part of life. But what if it doesn't have to be? What if the relentless activity of our thoughts is not an inherent condition but a habit we've unknowingly cultivated?

In this chapter, we explore the trap of thinking: why it happens, how it perpetuates itself, and what we can do to free ourselves from it. Through the insights of Zen masters and timeless spiritual teachings, we will uncover how the mind spins and how we can reclaim a deeper sense of peace by stepping off the mental merry-go-round.

The Mind as a Tool: A Double-Edged Sword

Thought is a necessary part of life. It allows us to plan, make decisions, solve problems, and reflect on our experiences. Without the ability to think, we would be unable to function in the world. However, the mind, like any tool, can become problematic when we allow it to run unchecked. Instead of using thought as a tool for specific tasks, we become trapped in an ongoing stream of mental activity.

Why does this happen? One reason lies in our evolutionary biology. Human beings evolved to think as a survival mechanism. Our ancestors had to constantly assess their environment, anticipate threats, and make decisions that would ensure their survival. Over time, this capacity for thought became more complex, allowing humans to build civilizations, create art, and advance

17

technology. But alongside these achievements, the human mind developed a tendency to overthink, even when survival wasn't at stake.

As a result, many of us live with an overactive mind, one that constantly generates thoughts—even when there's no immediate need for them. This endless stream of thought can become overwhelming, leading to stress, anxiety, and a sense of mental exhaustion. The mind, designed to help us navigate the world, becomes a double-edged sword: a powerful tool that can also trap us in cycles of unnecessary thinking.

Why Our Minds Spin: The Illusion of Safety

One of the primary reasons our minds continue to spin is because we believe that thinking will keep us safe. We think that by analyzing every possible outcome, by worrying about every potential problem, we can prevent negative things from happening. This is the mind's way of trying to exert control over the future, even though, in reality, the future is beyond our control.

Zen teachings emphasize that this illusion of control is one of the main sources of human suffering. When we try to control outcomes through thought, we create a false sense of security. But the reality is that no amount of thinking can prevent life's uncertainties. Zen Master Suzuki Roshi famously said,

"Leave your front door and your back door open. Allow your thoughts to come and go. Just don't serve them tea."

This teaching reminds us that while thoughts will always come and go, we don't need to attach ourselves to them or believe that they will provide us with control or safety.

The belief that thinking can protect us is deeply ingrained. For many of us, the act of thinking feels productive, as though by spinning ideas and scenarios in our minds, we are somehow taking action. However, this is rarely the case. Most of the time, thinking about a problem over and over does not lead to a solution; it only increases our anxiety and stress. The mind becomes trapped in a loop, endlessly spinning in an attempt to control the uncontrollable.

The Habit of Worry: Feeding the Mental Spin

Another reason our minds spin is because we have developed the habit of worrying. Worrying is often seen as a form of mental activity that prepares us for the worst, as if worrying will somehow prevent negative outcomes. But in truth, worry is a habit of the mind, and like all habits, it is one we can unlearn.

When we worry, we are not actually solving problems; we are simply feeding the mind's tendency to spin. Worry creates the illusion of control, but it doesn't lead to action. Instead, it keeps us trapped in a state of anxiety and fear. Zen Master Thich Nhat Hanh explains, "Worrying doesn't take away tomorrow's troubles, it takes away today's peace." This simple truth is often overlooked in our daily lives. When we worry, we are sacrificing our present peace of mind in exchange for an imagined future that may never come to pass.

Worrying can feel compulsive, like something we cannot stop. But with mindfulness, we can begin to see worry for what it is: a mental habit that arises from fear and uncertainty. By recognizing worry as a pattern of thought rather than an inevitable part of life, we can start to disengage from it. When we stop feeding worry with our attention, it begins to lose its power over us.

The Ego and Its Need for Reinforcement

The ego plays a significant role in keeping the mind spinning. The ego is that part of us that identifies with our thoughts, roles, and stories about who we are. It seeks constant reinforcement and validation, and it uses thought as a means of maintaining its sense of self. The ego thrives on comparison, judgment, and the need to feel separate from others.

When the ego is at the wheel, the mind is constantly generating thoughts that reinforce its identity. It may dwell on past achievements or failures, fantasize about future successes, or obsess over how others perceive us. The ego's primary concern is self-preservation, and it believes that by thinking, it can maintain its sense of importance and control.

However, the more we identify with the ego and its thoughts, the more trapped we become in the thinking trap. Zen Master Dogen teaches,

"When you let go of your habitual thoughts and allow
the mind to become empty, the original self appears,
free and clear."

This is a powerful reminder that our true self—the self that is free from the ego's demands—exists beyond the mind's constant spinning. To access this true self, we must learn to quiet the mind and disengage from the ego's need for validation.

The Role of Discontent: The Mind's Search for Satisfaction

One of the reasons our minds spin is because we are constantly searching for something to satisfy us. Whether it's a sense of accomplishment, recognition, or happiness, the mind is always looking for the next thing that will make us feel fulfilled. This search is often driven by a subtle sense of discontent—an underlying feeling that something is missing.

Zen teaches that this search for satisfaction is one of the main causes of suffering. When we are constantly looking for something outside ourselves to make us happy, we become trapped in a cycle of desire and frustration. The mind spins, trying to figure out what we need to do or achieve to feel complete, but no matter what we attain, the feeling of contentment is always fleeting.

Zen Master Shunryu Suzuki once said,

"When you realize that nothing is lacking, the whole world belongs to you."

This teaching points to the truth that contentment is not something we find through thinking or external achievement. It is something we experience when we stop searching and begin to appreciate the present moment as it is. When the mind stops spinning in its search for satisfaction, we can finally experience the peace and fulfillment that have always been available to us.

Breaking the Cycle of Overthinking: The Path to Freedom

So how do we break free from the thinking trap? The first step is awareness. We must become aware of when our minds are spinning, when we are caught in loops of worry, fear, or desire. Often, we are so accustomed to the constant activity of the mind that we don't even realize we are overthinking. By practicing mindfulness, we can begin to notice when the mind is engaged in unnecessary thinking and gently bring our attention back to the present moment.

Zen Master Thich Nhat Hanh teaches that mindfulness is the key to freeing ourselves from the trap of thought:

"The present moment is the only time over which we have dominion."

When we focus on the present moment—on our breath, our sensations, or the sounds around us—the mind begins to quiet. We step out of the stream of thought and into the stillness that exists beneath it.

The practice of mindfulness helps us to observe our thoughts without getting caught up in them. Instead of believing every thought that arises, we can learn to see them for what they are: temporary mental events that come and go. By developing this awareness, we create space between ourselves and our thoughts, and in that space, we find freedom.

The Art of Letting Go: Releasing Attachment to Thought

Another important aspect of breaking free from the thinking trap is learning to let go of our attachment to thought. Often, we become attached to certain thoughts or beliefs because they give us a sense of identity or security. We may hold onto thoughts of resentment, regret, or fear because we believe they define who we are. But in reality, our attachment to these thoughts only keeps us trapped in suffering.

Zen Master Dogen advises,

"Let go of your thoughts, and see the mind's true nature."

This teaching reminds us that the mind's true nature is not the constant activity of thought, but the stillness and clarity that exist beneath it. When we let go of our attachment to thought, we can experience the mind's natural state of peace and openness.

Letting go of thought does not mean suppressing or denying our thoughts. It means recognizing them for what they are—mental events that do not define us—and choosing not to engage with them. By practicing non-attachment, we free ourselves from the thinking trap and allow the mind to rest in stillness.

The Practice of Meditation: Cultivating a Quiet Mind

Meditation is one of the most effective practices for quieting the mind and breaking free from the thinking trap. Through meditation, we learn to observe our thoughts without getting caught up in them. We create a space of stillness where the mind can rest, and in that stillness, we begin to experience the peace that lies beyond thought.

Zen meditation, known as **zazen**, is a practice of sitting in silence and observing the mind. During zazen, thoughts naturally arise, but instead of following them, we simply let them pass. Over time, this practice helps us to disengage from the mind's constant activity and experience the deeper stillness that exists within us.

Zen Master Dogen describes zazen as

"sitting without thinking."

This practice is not about trying to stop thought, but about learning to let thought arise and pass without attachment. In this state of non-thinking, we experience the true nature of the mind—a mind that is clear, still, and free from the trap of overthinking.

Stepping Out of the Thinking Trap

The thinking trap is a powerful force that keeps us stuck in cycles of worry, fear, and striving. But as we have explored in this chapter, the mind's constant spinning is not an inescapable condition. Through mindfulness, non-attachment, and the practice of meditation, we can learn to quiet the mind and step out of the thinking trap.

As we continue on this journey, we will explore how these practices can be integrated into our daily lives, helping us to cultivate a sense of peace and clarity in everything we do. The mind may spin, but we are not powerless. With awareness and practice, we can find freedom from the thinking trap and experience the deep stillness that lies beyond thought.

CHAPTER 4

BATTLING THE NOISE: THOUGHTS VS. CONSCIOUS THINKING

The Symphony of Mental Noise

E ach day, we are bombarded by a cacophony of thoughts. These thoughts range from trivial matters—what we should eat for lunch, what someone said in a meeting, or how we look—to weightier concerns such as career decisions, family matters, or personal health. For many, this constant barrage feels like an inescapable mental noise, a loud background hum that follows us wherever we go.

While thoughts are a natural part of human experience, they often spiral into patterns of worry, judgment, and distraction. Amid this mental noise, how can we differentiate between the automatic, habitual thoughts that cloud our minds and conscious, purposeful thinking? The distinction between these two types of mental activity is critical for anyone seeking peace, clarity, and a more mindful life.

In this chapter, we will explore the difference between automatic thoughts and conscious thinking. We will delve into how habitual, uncontrolled thought patterns can lead to suffering, while intentional, conscious thinking can empower us. Drawing on the wisdom of Zen teachings, we will uncover practices to cultivate conscious thinking while letting go of unnecessary mental noise, so that we can achieve a more harmonious, centered way of being.

The Noise of Automatic Thoughts: The Default Mode of the Mind

For most of us, the majority of our thoughts arise automatically. These thoughts are a result of past conditioning, habitual mental patterns, and the brain's natural inclination to keep itself busy. Psychologists refer to this as the "default mode network"—the brain's tendency to wander when not engaged in a specific task. During these times, we often find ourselves lost in random thoughts, daydreams, or worry.

Automatic thoughts are not inherently negative. They often serve a purpose, such as alerting us to potential dangers or helping us solve problems. However, they can become problematic when we are not aware of them, allowing them to dominate our mental landscape without our conscious control. This mental noise can lead to overthinking, stress, and a sense of being mentally overwhelmed.

Zen Master Hakuin Zenji described the mind's tendency to generate thoughts automatically as

"the monkey mind."

The monkey mind swings from one thought to another, rarely staying still, and often leaving us exhausted. Hakuin wrote, "People have minds that race from one thought to the next like monkeys swinging from tree to tree." This analogy captures the chaotic, restless nature of automatic thinking, which prevents us from being fully present in the moment.

In contrast, conscious thinking involves intentional, focused thought. It requires awareness and mindfulness, allowing us to use the mind as a tool for specific purposes, rather than letting it run wild. But how do we tame the monkey mind? How do we break free from the trap of automatic thinking and reclaim the power of conscious thought?

Understanding the Nature of Conscious Thinking

Conscious thinking is not the absence of thought but the mindful engagement with it. When we engage in conscious thinking, we are aware of the thoughts we are having, and we are deliberately guiding them toward a particular goal or focus. This type of thinking is creative, intentional, and purposeful. It is the type of thinking we use when we are solving a problem, making a decision, or reflecting deeply on an issue.

Zen teachings often emphasize that true conscious thinking arises from a place of stillness and awareness. In this state, the mind is clear and calm, allowing thoughts to be purposeful rather than reactive. Conscious thinking is not driven by fear, worry, or judgment, but by clarity, curiosity, and understanding.

One of the most important aspects of conscious thinking is the ability to discern when a thought is helpful or unhelpful. Zen Master Seung Sahn taught,

"Our job is to understand what mind is. What is the thought? Where does it come from? What happens to it when it is finished?"

By asking ourselves these questions, we can begin to recognize the difference between mindless mental chatter and meaningful, conscious thought. Conscious thinking invites us to engage with thoughts in a way that serves us, rather than being swept away by the mind's automatic activity.

The Trap of Habitual Thought Patterns

Habitual thought patterns are one of the greatest obstacles to conscious thinking. These patterns develop over time through repetition and conditioning. For example, if you often worry about money, your brain may become conditioned to automatically generate thoughts of financial concern, even when there is no immediate need to worry. Over time, this becomes a habitual pattern, one that repeats itself without your conscious awareness or control.

These habitual patterns can be incredibly powerful because they reinforce themselves. The more you think about a particular issue—whether it's a worry, a regret, or a judgment—the stronger that mental pattern becomes. This is known as neuroplasticity, the brain's ability to rewire itself based on repeated experiences. While neuroplasticity can be beneficial when it comes to learning new skills or habits, it can also work against us when it strengthens negative or unhelpful thought patterns.

Zen Master Shunryu Suzuki explained this phenomenon when he said,

"As long as you seek for something, you will get the shadow of reality and not reality itself."

Habitual thinking often stems from a place of seeking—seeking control, seeking validation, seeking safety. But when we allow ourselves to be caught in these habitual patterns, we are not truly engaging with reality as it is. Instead, we are trapped in the mind's conditioned responses, unable to see clearly.

To break free from habitual thought patterns, we must first become aware of them. Mindfulness meditation is one of the most effective tools for cultivating this awareness. Through meditation, we learn to observe our thoughts without judgment, noticing when the mind has slipped into automatic thinking. By bringing awareness to these patterns, we can begin to dismantle them and replace them with more conscious, intentional thoughts.

The Role of Judgment in Mental Noise

Judgment is a common feature of automatic thinking, and it often contributes to the mental noise that fills our minds. We constantly judge ourselves, others, and the situations we encounter. This judgmental thinking is automatic and reactive—it arises without our conscious control, often based on past experiences, fears, or insecurities.

When we judge, we create a mental separation between ourselves and the world around us. We label things as "good" or "bad," "right" or "wrong," and in doing so, we reinforce a sense of division and conflict. This judgmental thinking not only creates suffering but also prevents us from engaging in conscious thought. Instead of seeing things as they are, we see them through the lens of our judgments.

Zen teachings emphasize the importance of letting go of judgment in order to experience true clarity and peace. As Zen Master Dogen said,

"Do not be concerned with the fault of others. Do not be obsessed by right and wrong."

This teaching invites us to release our attachment to judgment and instead approach each moment with an open, non-judgmental awareness.

When we let go of judgment, we create space for conscious thinking to arise. Instead of reacting automatically to situations with judgments, we can engage with them mindfully, asking ourselves questions such as, "What is truly happening in this moment?" and "How can I respond with awareness and compassion?" In this way, we move from automatic judgmental thinking to conscious, intentional thought.

Cultivating Awareness: The Path to Conscious Thinking

Awareness is the foundation of conscious thinking. Without awareness, we cannot recognize when the mind has slipped into automatic thinking, and we cannot choose to engage with our thoughts mindfully. Cultivating awareness is not a one-time event—it is an ongoing practice, one that requires patience, dedication, and mindfulness.

One of the most effective ways to cultivate awareness is through mindfulness meditation. In meditation, we practice observing our thoughts without getting caught up in them. This simple act of observation helps us develop the ability to step back from our thoughts and see them for what they are: temporary mental events that do not define us.

Zen Master Thich Nhat Hanh describes mindfulness as

"the energy of being aware and awake to the present moment."

When we are mindful, we are fully present with our thoughts, our emotions, and our surroundings. We are not lost in the past or the future, nor are we caught in the automatic patterns of the mind. Instead, we are fully engaged with what is happening right now, and from this place of awareness, conscious thinking can arise.

Practical Steps to Shift from Automatic to Conscious Thinking

While the concept of conscious thinking may sound abstract, it is something we can cultivate through daily practice. Here are several practical steps you can take to shift from automatic thinking to conscious thinking:

Practice Mindfulness Meditation: Set aside time each day to meditate. During meditation, focus on your breath and observe your thoughts as they arise. When you notice that your mind has wandered into automatic thinking, gently bring your attention back to your breath. Over time, this practice will help you become more aware of your thoughts and more skilled at disengaging from automatic thinking.

Question Your Thoughts: When you notice that you are caught in automatic thinking, pause and ask yourself, "Is this thought helpful? Is it true? Is it necessary?" By questioning your thoughts, you can begin to discern which thoughts are worth engaging with and which ones are simply mental noise.

Practice Non-Judgment: When you find yourself judging yourself or others, take a moment to pause and bring awareness to the judgment. Ask yourself, "What is behind this judgment? Am I reacting out of fear, insecurity, or past conditioning?" By bringing awareness to judgmental thinking, you can begin to let go of it and replace it with more compassionate, conscious thought.

Engage in Purposeful Reflection: Set aside time each day for conscious thinking. This could involve reflecting on your goals, solving a problem, or simply contemplating a meaningful question. During this time, focus your thoughts on the task at hand and resist the urge to let your mind wander. This practice will help you strengthen your ability to engage in conscious, intentional thinking.

Embrace Stillness: Conscious thinking often arises from a place of stillness and calm. Make time in your day to simply be still. This could involve sitting quietly, taking a walk in nature, or practicing deep breathing. In moments of stillness, the mind's automatic noise begins to quiet, and conscious thinking can emerge.

The Wisdom of Zen: Integrating Conscious Thinking into Daily Life

Zen teachings provide us with valuable insights into how we can integrate conscious thinking into our daily lives. At the heart of Zen practice is the idea that true clarity and wisdom arise from a quiet, still mind. When the mind is filled with noise, we are unable to see clearly or think consciously. But when we cultivate stillness and mindfulness, we can engage with our thoughts in a way that is intentional, creative, and purposeful.

Zen Master Huang Po once said, "Do not permit the events of your daily life to bind you, but never withdraw yourself from them." This teaching reminds us that conscious thinking is not about withdrawing from life or escaping its challenges. Instead, it is about engaging with life fully, but from a place of clarity and awareness. When we approach life with a quiet, mindful mind, we are able to think consciously and respond to situations with wisdom and compassion.

The Dance Between Thoughts and Conscious Thinking

The battle between automatic thoughts and conscious thinking is a fundamental aspect of the human experience. While we cannot completely eliminate automatic thinking, we can learn to cultivate awareness and mindfulness, allowing us to engage with our thoughts in a more conscious, intentional way. By letting go of habitual thought patterns, judgment, and mental noise, we create space for conscious thinking to arise—thinking that is grounded in clarity, compassion, and presence.

As we continue on this journey, we will explore how the practices of mindfulness, meditation, and non-judgment can help us deepen our ability to think consciously. The mind is a powerful tool, and when used with awareness, it has the potential to bring us greater peace, fulfillment, and wisdom.

CHAPTER 5

BEYOND POSITIVITY
FEELING WITHOUT THE NEED TO CONTROL

The Search for Positivity

I n modern culture, we are constantly encouraged to "think positive" and "look on the bright side," as if the only valid approach to life is to embrace optimism at every turn. Social media, self-help literature, and even well-meaning friends and family push the idea that if we simply adopt a positive mindset, we can conquer all challenges and avoid discomfort. While positivity can be a powerful tool, an overemphasis on being constantly positive can become limiting and even harmful. It can cause us to suppress or avoid emotions that don't fit the "positive" mold, creating a disconnection from our true selves.

This chapter will explore the complexities of emotional life, arguing that true peace comes not from forcing ourselves to feel a certain way but from allowing ourselves to feel fully—without the need to control or manipulate our emotions. We'll investigate how the obsession with positivity can backfire, leading to emotional repression, and we'll explore practices for embracing all emotions with compassion, even those we typically avoid. Drawing from Zen teachings and contemporary psychological insights, this chapter will guide you toward emotional freedom by helping you release the need to control your feelings.

The Downside of Positivity: When It Becomes an Obsession

At first glance, positivity seems like an entirely good thing. After all, who wouldn't want to focus on the brighter aspects of life? However, the relentless pursuit of positivity can actually lead us to deny or minimize real emotions that don't fit the optimistic narrative. This is what has come to be known as **toxic positivity**—the insistence on maintaining a positive mindset even when facing serious challenges or genuine emotional pain.

Toxic positivity pushes us to reject or repress any feelings that are deemed negative, such as sadness, anger, frustration, or fear. In doing so, it creates a false dichotomy where emotions are categorized as either good or bad. When we label emotions in this way, we make it difficult for ourselves to accept and process the full range of human experience. Instead of allowing ourselves to feel and process our emotions, we mask them with forced optimism, which can lead to emotional numbness or an inability to cope with life's complexities.

Many people may feel guilty when they experience emotions like sadness or anger, believing that they're failing to uphold the positive mindset they've been told is the key to happiness. However, by clinging to positivity at all costs, we close ourselves off from the lessons and growth that can come from fully experiencing and understanding all of our emotions.

The Need for Emotional Authenticity

Rather than striving for constant positivity, it is far more important to cultivate emotional **authenticity**—the ability to fully acknowledge and experience whatever emotions arise, without judgment or suppression. Authenticity doesn't mean indulging in negative emotions or being swept away by them, but rather allowing them to be felt without resistance.

Zen teachings often emphasize the importance of accepting the present moment as it is, without trying to force it into a particular shape. Similarly, accepting our emotions as they arise—whether they are pleasant or painful—frees us from the mental and emotional tension created by resistance. By letting go of the need to be positive all the time, we open ourselves to a more nuanced, honest, and ultimately peaceful emotional life.

Zen Master Thich Nhat Hanh teaches that

"To live in the present moment is a miracle."

This applies to our emotional experiences as well. When we are fully present with our emotions, we can experience them authentically, without the need to mold them into something else. This presence allows us to process emotions in a healthy, non-reactive way, leading to greater emotional resilience over time.

Why We Try to Control Emotions

At the heart of our struggle with emotions is the desire for control. Many of us believe that if we can manage or control our emotions, we can avoid suffering and keep life within manageable limits. This need for control is deeply ingrained in our culture, where emotional displays are often seen as weaknesses, and people are praised for their ability to remain calm and composed no matter what they're feeling inside.

However, this desire for control is based on the false premise that emotions are problems to be solved rather than experiences to be lived. Emotions are not things we can easily turn off or manipulate to fit our preferences. Instead, they are dynamic, fluid experiences that arise as natural responses to our environment, thoughts, and relationships.

Our efforts to control emotions often lead to emotional repression, which can have harmful consequences over time. When we suppress or ignore difficult emotions, we prevent ourselves from understanding and integrating them. Unprocessed emotions remain buried within us, leading to stress, anxiety, and even physical ailments.

By trying to control our emotions, we essentially deny our humanity. To feel deeply—both the joys and the sorrows of life—is part of what makes us human. When we resist emotions, we cut ourselves off from the full richness of life, limiting our ability to experience connection, empathy, and growth.

The Role of Fear in Emotional Control

One of the primary reasons we try to control our emotions is fear. Many of us fear negative emotions, believing that if we let them in, they will overwhelm us. We may be afraid of the intensity of sadness, anger, or fear, or we may worry that if we allow ourselves to feel these emotions, we will lose control and spiral into despair.

This fear of negative emotions is understandable but ultimately misguided. Emotions, by their very nature, are transient. They arise, peak, and then pass. When we try to control or suppress them, we only prolong the process, creating a kind of emotional stalemate where we are stuck in a cycle of avoidance.

Zen teaches us to face our fears, not to run from them. The great Zen master Linji Yixuan said,

"Do not seek for the truth; only cease to cherish opinions."

This teaching reminds us that much of our suffering comes not from the emotions themselves but from the opinions and judgments we hold about them. When we fear our emotions, we label them as bad or dangerous, and this judgment amplifies our suffering. By letting go of these judgments, we can experience our emotions fully without being consumed by them.

Beyond Positivity: The Power of Acceptance

If we move beyond the idea that emotions need to be controlled or categorized into positive and negative, we can begin to approach emotions with a mindset of acceptance. Acceptance is not the same as resignation or passivity. It doesn't mean we have to like every emotion we experience, but it does mean that we allow ourselves to feel emotions without trying to change, avoid, or suppress them.

Acceptance can be incredibly freeing. When we stop trying to control our emotions and instead allow them to move through us naturally, we release a great deal of tension and anxiety. We realize that emotions are not as scary or overwhelming as we once believed. They are simply part of the flow of life.

Zen Master Dogen wrote,

"When you walk, just walk. When you sit, just sit; but above all, don't wobble."

This simple teaching reminds us of the importance of being fully present in whatever we are doing, without getting caught up in distraction or resistance. The same principle applies to our emotional life: when we feel an emotion, we should allow ourselves to feel it fully without trying to wobble—without resisting, avoiding, or controlling it.

The Wisdom of Equanimity

One of the most valuable qualities we can cultivate when it comes to our emotional life is **equanimity**—the ability to remain steady and balanced in the face of life's inevitable ups and downs. Equanimity does not mean that we don't feel emotions, but rather that we don't allow ourselves to be carried away by them. It is the ability to experience emotions fully without being overwhelmed by them.

Equanimity is rooted in the understanding that emotions, like all things in life, are impermanent. When we experience a joyful moment, it will eventually pass. When we experience sorrow, it too will pass. By developing equanimity, we learn to navigate life's emotional highs and lows with grace and poise, trusting in the natural ebb and flow of experience.

Zen practice teaches that equanimity comes from a deep understanding of **impermanence**. When we recognize that all emotions are temporary, we stop clinging to positive emotions and resisting negative ones. Instead, we can remain open to whatever arises, knowing that it will eventually change. This sense of openness and acceptance is the essence of equanimity.

Embracing the Full Emotional Spectrum

The goal of emotional freedom is not to eliminate negative emotions or to remain in a constant state of positivity. Rather, it is to embrace the full spectrum of emotions with openness and acceptance. Life is rich with both joy and sorrow, pleasure and pain, success and failure. To fully engage with life means to experience all of these emotions without resistance.

When we embrace the full spectrum of emotions, we develop a deeper connection to ourselves and to others. We become more compassionate, both toward ourselves and toward those around us. We recognize that emotions are not something to be controlled or feared, but something to be understood and felt. In this way, we move beyond the limitations of toxic positivity and enter into a more authentic, fulfilling way of being.

Zen Master Dogen once said,

*"You should realize that the practice exists before you,
and you have to step into it."*

This teaching invites us to understand that the path to emotional freedom is not something that can be forced or controlled—it is something we must step into with openness and curiosity. When we do so, we find that the practice of accepting our emotions as they are is already available to us. We just have to allow ourselves to experience it.

How to Cultivate Emotional Freedom: Practical Steps

Moving beyond the need for control and embracing the full spectrum of emotions is a practice that requires mindfulness, patience, and self-compassion. Here are some practical steps you can take to begin cultivating emotional freedom:

1. **Practice Mindfulness of Emotions**: Spend a few minutes each day practicing mindfulness of your emotions. When an emotion arises, simply observe it without judgment. Notice how it feels in your body and how it shifts over time. Allow the emotion to be there without trying to control or change it.

2. **Let Go of Labels**: Resist the urge to label emotions as "good" or "bad." Instead, view emotions as neutral experiences that arise and pass. By letting go of labels, you can experience emotions without the added layer of judgment or resistance.

3. **Embrace Impermanence**: Remind yourself that all emotions are temporary. When you are experiencing a difficult emotion, take a few deep breaths and remind yourself that this too shall pass. When you are experiencing a joyful moment, savor it without clinging to it, knowing that it will eventually change.

4. **Cultivate Self-Compassion**: When challenging emotions arise, offer yourself compassion. Acknowledge that it's okay to feel whatever you are feeling, and remind yourself that all emotions are part of the human experience. Treat yourself with kindness and understanding, just as you would treat a friend going through a difficult time.

5. **Practice Equanimity**: Throughout the day, practice maintaining a sense of inner balance, even in the face of emotional highs and lows. When a difficult emotion arises, remind yourself to stay grounded and centered, trusting that it will pass. When a positive emotion arises, allow yourself to enjoy it without clinging to it.

Emotional Freedom Beyond Control

In this chapter, we have explored the limitations of toxic positivity and the deeper emotional freedom that comes from feeling without the need to control. By embracing the full range of emotions with openness and acceptance, we can move beyond the superficial pursuit of positivity and into a more authentic, balanced way of being.

Zen teachings remind us that life is filled with both joy and sorrow, and that true peace comes not from controlling our emotions but from accepting them. When we let go of the need for control, we free ourselves from the tension and anxiety that arise from resistance. We learn to trust in the natural flow of life, allowing our emotions to arise and pass like waves in the ocean.

As we continue on this journey, we will explore how to integrate these practices into our daily lives, cultivating a deeper sense of peace, equanimity, and emotional freedom. By moving beyond the need to control, we open ourselves to the richness of the human experience, allowing ourselves to feel fully and live more authentically.

CHAPTER 6

THE CREATION OF YOUR REALITY
THE THREE PILLARS OF EXPERIENCE

The Power of Perception

T he world we experience is not an objective reality shared identically by everyone but is shaped by our perceptions, beliefs, and thoughts. Two people can look at the same event or circumstance and experience it in entirely different ways. What makes one person see a challenge as an opportunity while another feels paralyzed by fear? How do we create the reality we live in, and more importantly, how can we consciously shape it in ways that bring peace, joy, and fulfillment?

The answer lies in understanding the three foundational pillars that shape our experience: **thoughts, emotions, and perceptions**. These three elements interact continuously, forming the lens through which we interpret and respond to the world around us. In this chapter, we will explore how these pillars create our reality and how, by becoming aware of them, we can shift from reacting unconsciously to life to consciously creating a reality that aligns with our deepest values and desires.

The First Pillar: Thoughts as Architects of Reality

The first and most fundamental pillar of our experience is our thoughts. Our thoughts form the architecture of the reality we perceive. They frame how we interpret events, how we see ourselves, and how we interact with the world. Often, we are unaware of the pervasive influence our thoughts have on our experience because they are constant and automatic. Yet, every thought we think is shaping the story we tell ourselves about reality.

Zen Master Thich Nhat Hanh once said,

*"Your mind is like a garden. It can grow compassion or
fear, resentment or love. With the right attention, it
can blossom into beauty."*

This quote illustrates the power of our thoughts to shape the emotional and experiential landscape of our lives. Just as a garden grows what we plant in it, our minds produce the experiences we cultivate through our thoughts. If we are constantly planting seeds of worry, judgment, or fear, those are the plants that will flourish. Conversely, when we consciously cultivate thoughts of kindness, gratitude, and understanding, we begin to shift the narrative of our lives.

Thoughts are not neutral; they carry energy. Negative thoughts have a way of reinforcing themselves, creating a cycle that perpetuates stress, anxiety, or feelings of inadequacy. Similarly, positive or mindful thoughts also reinforce themselves, creating a sense of ease, clarity, and well-being. The key is to recognize the thoughts that dominate our inner world and understand their role in shaping our experience.

One of the fundamental principles in Zen practice is to observe thoughts without attachment. The more we can detach from the content of our thoughts and simply observe them, the less power they hold over us. We begin to see that thoughts are transient—they arise, linger for a moment, and then dissolve. By recognizing this impermanence, we can avoid becoming overly identified with the thoughts that pass through our minds. This is where conscious thinking begins: with the awareness that we can choose which thoughts to engage with and which to let go of.

The Impact of Belief Systems on Thought Patterns

Our thoughts do not exist in isolation. They are shaped and influenced by the belief systems we hold—both conscious and unconscious. These beliefs form the core of our thought patterns and often dictate how we interpret reality. For example, if you hold a belief that the world is inherently dangerous, your thoughts will likely focus on potential threats and uncertainties. On the other hand, if you believe that life is full of opportunities, your thoughts will be more oriented toward possibility and growth.

Beliefs are often passed down through culture, family, and personal experiences, and they tend to operate automatically in the background, influencing our thoughts without us even realizing it. The first step in transforming your reality is to examine the belief systems that are driving your thought patterns. What do you believe about yourself? What do you believe about the world? And are these beliefs serving you or holding you back?

In Zen, there is a strong emphasis on letting go of fixed beliefs and adopting a mindset of openness and inquiry. Zen Master Shunryu Suzuki famously said,

"In the beginner's mind there are many possibilities,
but in the expert's mind there are few."

This teaching reminds us that rigid beliefs can limit our thinking and our experience of reality. By adopting a "beginner's mind," we open ourselves to new ways of seeing the world and new possibilities for creating our reality.

The Second Pillar: Emotions as Catalysts of Experience

While thoughts are the architects of our reality, emotions are the catalysts that bring those thoughts to life. Emotions give our experiences color and intensity, transforming abstract thoughts into lived experience. Whether we realize it or not, emotions play a powerful role in shaping the reality we perceive and create.

For example, imagine you're walking through a park on a sunny day. If you're feeling joyful, you'll likely notice the beauty of the trees, the warmth of the sun, and the sound of birds singing. If you're feeling anxious or sad, you might be more attuned to the noise of traffic in the distance or the dirt on the path. The same external environment is present, but your emotional state dictates how you experience it.

Emotions are not inherently good or bad, but they can influence how we interpret the world around us. When we become aware of the emotions we are experiencing, we gain insight into how they are shaping our perception of reality. Instead of allowing emotions to control us, we can learn to observe them, understand them, and choose how to respond.

Zen practice provides valuable methods for nurturing emotional awareness and balance. Through mindfulness, we can witness our emotions as they emerge, giving ourselves the opportunity to pause before reacting impulsively. This mindful observation creates a gap between stimulus and response, allowing for thoughtful, intentional reactions rather than automatic ones. As Zen Master Dogen expressed,

"The Way is essentially perfect and all-pervading. How
could it be contingent upon practice and realization?"

In terms of our emotions, this teaching suggests that when we observe our feelings without becoming entangled in them, we access a deeper state of clarity and tranquility.

Emotions as Energy in Motion

The word "emotion" itself suggests movement—**"energy in motion."** Emotions are dynamic and fluid, and they are meant to be experienced and released, not suppressed or controlled. However, many of us have learned to resist or avoid certain emotions, especially those that are uncomfortable or painful. When we suppress emotions, they don't disappear; they remain stored in the body and can manifest in physical or psychological symptoms over time.

The practice of allowing emotions to flow freely without attachment or judgment is central to Zen. Instead of labeling emotions as good or bad, we can learn to see them as natural expressions of life's unfolding. When we stop trying to control or resist our emotions, we allow them to move through us, creating a sense of emotional freedom and balance.

By embracing the full range of emotions, we create a richer, more authentic experience of reality. We are no longer limited by the need to feel only positive emotions; instead, we can feel deeply and fully, knowing that all emotions have value and are part of the human experience.

The Third Pillar: Perception as the Lens of Reality

The third pillar of experience is **perception**, which acts as the lens through which we view the world. Our perceptions are shaped by our thoughts and emotions, but they are also influenced by our sensory experiences—what we see, hear, taste, touch, and smell. Perception is how we interpret the raw data of the external world, and it plays a critical role in shaping our reality.

While perception is often thought of as something that happens automatically, it is actually a dynamic process that can be influenced by our awareness and intention. For example, two people can perceive the same event in entirely different ways based on their emotional state, thoughts, and past experiences. This is why perception is not a fixed or objective reality—it is shaped by the internal landscape of the perceiver.

Zen emphasizes the importance of cultivating clear perception. Through mindfulness and meditation, we can learn to see things as they are, without the distortion of preconceived notions or habitual thought patterns. When we see clearly, we are able to respond to life with wisdom and compassion, rather than reacting out of fear or judgment.

Zen Master Hakuin Zenji taught,

"From the beginning, all beings are Buddha."

This teaching points to the idea that our true nature is inherently clear and awakened, but our perceptions are often clouded by the distractions and delusions of the mind. By practicing mindfulness and meditation, we can clear the lens of perception, allowing us to experience reality in its purest form.

The Interplay of Thoughts, Emotions, and Perceptions

While we have explored each pillar of experience individually—thoughts, emotions, and perceptions—it's important to recognize that these three elements are deeply interconnected. Our thoughts influence our emotions, our emotions shape our perceptions, and our perceptions reinforce our thoughts. Together, they create a feedback loop that continually shapes our experience of reality.

For example, if you have the thought, "I'm not good enough," this thought may trigger feelings of sadness or inadequacy. Those emotions, in turn, may affect how you perceive the world—you may begin to see challenges as insurmountable or believe that others are judging you. This reinforces the original thought, creating a cycle that can be difficult to break.

The good news is that by becoming aware of this interplay, we can begin to consciously shift our experience. When we notice a negative thought, we can question its validity and choose a more empowering thought. When we experience difficult emotions, we can allow ourselves to feel them fully without judgment, trusting that they will pass. And by cultivating clear perception, we can see reality more accurately, without the distortions of fear or insecurity.

Creating Your Reality: Conscious Choice and Intention

The key to creating your reality lies in conscious choice and intention. While much of our experience is shaped by automatic thoughts, emotions, and perceptions, we have the power to become more intentional about how we engage with these elements. By practicing mindfulness and self-awareness, we can begin to make conscious choices about how we think, feel, and perceive the world.

Zen practice offers a path for cultivating this awareness. Through meditation, we learn to quiet the mind and observe our inner landscape without attachment. This allows us to see the patterns that shape our reality and gives us the space to make different choices. Instead of reacting unconsciously to life, we can respond with clarity and intention.

As we become more conscious of the three pillars of experience, we can begin to align our thoughts, emotions, and perceptions with our highest values and intentions. This doesn't mean that we will never experience negative thoughts or emotions, but it does mean that we can approach them with greater awareness and equanimity. We can choose how we respond to life, rather than being at the mercy of automatic reactions.

Zen Wisdom on Creating Your Reality

Zen teachings provide valuable insights into how we can consciously create our reality. Zen Master Dogen wrote,

*"To be in harmony with the oneness of things is to be
without anxiety about imperfection."*

This teaching reminds us that creating our reality is not about controlling every aspect of life or striving for perfection. Instead, it is about being in harmony with the present moment and accepting life as it is.

When we approach life with this sense of harmony and acceptance, we are able to create a reality that is grounded in peace, compassion, and understanding. We are no longer driven by the need to control or manipulate our experience; instead, we can trust in the natural flow of life and respond with wisdom and grace.

Practical Steps for Creating Your Reality

Creating your reality is an ongoing practice that requires mindfulness, self-awareness, and intention. Here are some practical steps to help you align your thoughts, emotions, and perceptions with the reality you want to create:

1. **Mindfulness Meditation**: Set aside time each day to practice mindfulness meditation. During meditation, observe your thoughts and emotions without judgment. Notice how they shape your

perception of the world, and practice letting go of thoughts and emotions that no longer serve you.

2. **Examine Your Beliefs**: Take time to reflect on the belief systems that are driving your thoughts. Are these beliefs empowering or limiting? Question the validity of beliefs that hold you back and consider adopting more expansive, open-minded beliefs.

3. **Cultivate Emotional Awareness**: Throughout the day, check in with your emotional state. Are your emotions influencing how you perceive the world? Practice allowing emotions to arise and pass without attachment, and notice how this shifts your experience.

4. **Practice Clear Perception**: Make an effort to see things as they are, without the distortion of preconceived notions or judgments. When you find yourself making assumptions about a situation, pause and ask yourself, "Is this perception accurate, or is it influenced by my thoughts or emotions?"

5. **Set Intentions**: Each day, set clear intentions for how you want to engage with the world. Whether it's cultivating more compassion, practicing gratitude, or approaching challenges with curiosity, setting intentions helps guide your thoughts, emotions, and perceptions in a positive direction.

The Power of Creation

In this chapter, we have explored the three pillars of experience—thoughts, emotions, and perceptions—and how they shape the reality we live in. By becoming aware of these pillars and practicing mindfulness, we can consciously create a reality that aligns with our highest values and intentions. The power to create your reality lies within you, and through awareness and intention, you can transform your experience of life.

Zen teachings remind us that life is not something to be controlled or manipulated but something to be experienced fully, with presence and acceptance. As we continue on this journey, we will explore how to integrate these practices into our daily lives, helping us cultivate greater peace, clarity, and harmony.

By aligning your thoughts, emotions, and perceptions with your true self, you open the door to a life that is rich with meaning and connection—a life that reflects the reality you wish to create.

CHAPTER 7

BREAKING FREE
HOW TO END THE CYCLE OF
OVERTHINKING

The Trap of Overthinking

Overthinking is a familiar experience for most of us. It is that persistent mental chatter, the constant replaying of past events, the obsessive planning for future scenarios, and the analysis of every possible outcome, often leading to stress, anxiety, and emotional exhaustion. At first glance, thinking deeply about situations might seem like a strength—after all, isn't contemplation necessary for making good decisions? But when our thinking becomes compulsive and repetitive, it can trap us in an endless loop, preventing us from finding clarity and peace.

In this chapter, we will explore the cycle of overthinking: what causes it, why it's so difficult to escape, and how we can break free from its grip. Through the lens of mindfulness and Zen teachings, we will uncover practical strategies for quieting the mind, letting go of obsessive thought patterns, and reclaiming a sense of calm and mental stillness. Drawing from ancient wisdom and modern psychological insights, we will learn how to cultivate a state of presence that transcends the need to analyze, worry, or control every aspect of our lives.

Understanding the Nature of Overthinking

Overthinking can be defined as the habit of excessively dwelling on thoughts to the point that it disrupts our ability to take action, make decisions, or experience peace. It often involves rumination on the past or excessive worry about the future, with little connection to the present moment. The cycle of overthinking typically begins with a single thought, but that thought triggers more thoughts, leading to a chain reaction that spirals into mental clutter.

Why do we overthink? One reason is the brain's natural desire to solve problems. The human mind is wired for problem-solving, and when faced with uncertainty, it instinctively tries to generate solutions by thinking through every possible outcome. While this can be helpful in certain situations, it becomes problematic when the mind becomes stuck in this problem-solving mode, even when there's no immediate issue to address. Overthinking, in this sense, is the mind's attempt to gain control over the uncontrollable aspects of life.

Another cause of overthinking is fear. We overthink because we are afraid of making the wrong decision, afraid of what others might think, or afraid of the uncertainty that the future holds. By continuously analyzing situations, we hope to mitigate this fear, but in reality, overthinking only magnifies it. Instead of finding solutions, we become more entangled in doubt and worry.

Zen Master Takuan Soho offers a perspective on overthinking:

"The mind must always be in the state of 'flowing,' for when it stops anywhere, that means the flow is interrupted, and it is this interruption that is injurious to the well-being of the mind."

In this context, overthinking is the result of the mind stopping or fixating on certain thoughts rather than allowing them to pass naturally. When we become stuck in thought, the flow of mental energy is disrupted, leading to mental fatigue and emotional suffering.

The Illusion of Control Through Thinking

One of the primary reasons we fall into the trap of overthinking is the illusion that by thinking more, we can gain control over our circumstances. We believe that if we analyze a situation from every angle, we can predict and prevent negative outcomes. This creates a false sense of security, as though thinking deeply will protect us from uncertainty or failure.

However, life is inherently unpredictable. No matter how much we think, plan, or analyze, we cannot control every variable. Overthinking doesn't prevent bad things from happening; it simply keeps us stuck in a loop of mental paralysis. By trying to think our way out of uncertainty, we only end up amplifying our sense of fear and helplessness.

Zen practice teaches us to release the need for control and embrace the present moment as it is. Instead of trying to manipulate or control the future through overthinking, we can learn to trust the natural flow of life. As Zen Master Shunryu Suzuki explains, "In the beginner's mind there are many possibilities, but in the expert's mind there are few." This quote highlights the

45

openness and receptivity that come from letting go of rigid thought patterns and embracing the unknown.

The Role of Perfectionism in Overthinking

Perfectionism is another significant contributor to overthinking. Those who struggle with perfectionism often feel that they must think through every detail of a situation to ensure the "perfect" outcome. This leads to excessive planning, worrying, and second-guessing, as the perfectionist mind seeks to avoid any mistake or imperfection.

Perfectionism and overthinking feed into each other in a destructive cycle. The more we overthink, the more we feel the need to perfect our thoughts, decisions, and actions. And the more we strive for perfection, the more we overthink to avoid failure. This cycle can become exhausting and debilitating, leading to indecision, procrastination, and a deep sense of inadequacy.

Zen wisdom offers a path out of this cycle by teaching us to embrace imperfection as a natural part of life. In the Japanese aesthetic of **wabi-sabi**, imperfection is seen as beautiful and meaningful. Instead of striving for unattainable perfection, we can learn to appreciate the flaws and imperfections that make life—and ourselves—unique.

The Zen practice of letting go of perfectionism is encapsulated in the concept of **zazen**, or seated meditation. In zazen, there is no goal to achieve, no perfect way to meditate. The practice is simply to sit and be present with whatever arises, without judgment or expectation. This acceptance of imperfection in meditation can be carried into daily life, helping us to break free from the need to overthink in the pursuit of perfection.

How Overthinking Impacts Emotional and Mental Health

The cycle of overthinking takes a toll not only on our mental clarity but also on our emotional and physical well-being. Prolonged overthinking can lead to increased levels of stress and anxiety, as the mind becomes overwhelmed by constant analysis and worry. This can manifest in physical symptoms such as tension headaches, fatigue, digestive issues, and disrupted sleep patterns.

Emotionally, overthinking can create a sense of powerlessness and frustration. When we are caught in the loop of overthinking, we feel as though we are spinning our wheels without making any progress. This can lead to feelings of inadequacy, self-doubt, and even depression. The more we try to think our way out of a situation, the more stuck we become.

The mind's tendency to overthink also impacts our relationships. When we are preoccupied with our thoughts, we are less present with others. We may find ourselves disengaged from conversations or distracted during important moments. Overthinking can also lead to misunderstandings in relationships, as we analyze every word or action, often misinterpreting the intentions of others.

Zen practice encourages us to bring mindfulness and presence to our relationships. By being fully present with others, we can let go of the mental chatter and engage in authentic connection. As Zen Master Thich Nhat Hanh advises,

> "When you love someone, the best thing you can offer
> is your presence. How can you love if you are not
> there?"

This teaching reminds us that by being present, we not only free ourselves from overthinking but also deepen our relationships with others.

Breaking Free from the Cycle of Overthinking

Breaking free from overthinking requires both mindfulness and intention. It is not enough to simply will ourselves to stop overthinking; we must develop practices that help us quiet the mind and bring awareness to our thought patterns. Below are several strategies for ending the cycle of overthinking and cultivating a more peaceful, present state of mind.

1. Mindfulness Meditation

Mindfulness meditation is one of the most effective tools for quieting the mind and breaking the cycle of overthinking. In mindfulness meditation, we practice observing our thoughts without judgment or attachment. Instead of getting caught up in the content of our thoughts, we simply notice them as they arise and let them pass.

Through regular meditation, we develop the ability to create space between ourselves and our thoughts. This space allows us to see that we are not our thoughts and that we do not have to engage with every thought that arises. Over time, this practice helps us to break the habit of overthinking and cultivate a sense of mental clarity and calm.

2. Focus on the Present Moment

Overthinking is often fueled by a preoccupation with the past or the future. We replay past events, wondering what we could have done differently, or we worry about future outcomes that are beyond our control. To break free from this cycle, it is essential to bring our attention back to the present moment.

Zen practice emphasizes the importance of living in the present. As Zen Master Dogen wrote,

"Do not think you will necessarily be aware of your own enlightenment."

This teaching reminds us that enlightenment, or peace, is not something we achieve in the future; it is something we experience in the present moment. By focusing on the here and now, we can quiet the mind and let go of the need to overthink.

One practical way to bring attention to the present moment is through mindful breathing. By focusing on the rhythm of our breath, we anchor ourselves in the present and create a sense of calm. Whenever we notice our mind wandering into overthinking, we can return to the breath and ground ourselves in the present.

3. Question Your Thoughts

One of the reasons we overthink is that we believe every thought that passes through our minds. However, not all thoughts are accurate or helpful. In fact, many of our thoughts are distorted by fear, doubt, or past conditioning. To break free from overthinking, it's important to question the validity of our thoughts.

When you find yourself caught in overthinking, ask yourself: **Is this thought true? Is it helpful? What evidence do I have to support it?** By challenging the assumptions behind your thoughts, you can begin to see them more objectively and release the need to overthink.

Letting Go of Overthinking Through Acceptance

One of the most powerful ways to break free from overthinking is to cultivate acceptance. Overthinking often arises from a desire to control outcomes or avoid uncertainty. We believe that if we think enough, we can prevent bad things from happening or ensure that everything turns out perfectly. But this is an illusion. Life is full of uncertainty, and no amount of thinking can change that.

By accepting the uncertainty of life, we can let go of the need to overthink. Zen teachings emphasize the importance of accepting life as it is, without attachment or resistance. When we embrace the impermanence and unpredictability of life, we free ourselves from the mental and emotional burden of overthinking.

Zen Master Hakuin Zenji taught,

"Meditation in the midst of activity is a thousand times superior to meditation in stillness."

This teaching reminds us that acceptance is not something we practice only in moments of stillness or meditation; it is something we carry with us into the chaos and uncertainty of daily life. By practicing acceptance in every moment, we can release the need to overthink and experience greater peace.

Practical Exercises for Breaking Free from Overthinking

To integrate the insights from this chapter into your daily life, consider practicing the following exercises designed to help you break free from the cycle of overthinking:

1. Thought Observation Journal

Keep a journal where you record the thoughts that arise when you catch yourself overthinking. Write down the thought and ask yourself the following questions:

- Is this thought based on fact or fear?

- Is it helpful or harmful?

- What action, if any, can I take in response to this thought?

By journaling your thoughts, you can bring greater awareness to your thought patterns and begin to discern which thoughts are worth engaging with and which are simply mental noise.

2. Mindful Walking

Practice mindful walking as a way to bring yourself into the present moment and quiet the mind. As you walk, focus your attention on the sensations of your body—the feeling of your feet touching the ground, the movement of your legs, and the rhythm of your breath. Whenever your mind starts to wander into overthinking, gently bring your attention back to the physical sensations of walking.

Mindful walking helps to break the cycle of overthinking by grounding you in the present moment and providing a physical outlet for mental energy.

3. The One-Thought Practice

Throughout the day, whenever you notice yourself caught in overthinking, practice the "one-thought" technique. Focus your mind on a single thought or object, such as your breath, a mantra, or a simple task at hand. By concentrating on one thing at a time, you can quiet the mental chatter and bring clarity to your thoughts.

Finding Freedom Beyond Thought

Breaking free from the cycle of overthinking is not about suppressing or eliminating thoughts but about developing a mindful relationship with them. By observing our thoughts without attachment, practicing presence, and cultivating acceptance, we can release the mental habits that keep us stuck in overthinking and experience a greater sense of peace and clarity.

Zen teachings remind us that true freedom lies not in controlling every thought but in letting go of the need to control. As we continue on this journey, we will explore how to apply these principles in everyday life, helping us cultivate a deeper connection to the present moment and a more peaceful, centered way of being.

CHAPTER 8

FLOURISHING WITHOUT THOUGHT EMBRACE MINDFUL PRESENCE

The Silence Beneath the Noise

Picture this: the constant mental chatter that accompanies you from morning until night—the plans, the worries, the what-ifs—slows down. The world doesn't disappear, but instead, it becomes more vivid, more alive. You notice the softness of the breeze, the distant laughter of children, the steady beat of your own heart. In this moment, you are not distracted by a thousand thoughts racing through your mind. You are simply *here*—fully present, fully alive.

This is the essence of flourishing without thought. It's not about shutting down your thinking mind or becoming passive; it's about learning to be in the world with greater clarity and presence. It's about engaging with life more fully by stepping out of the relentless stream of thoughts that often dictate our actions and perceptions. When we do this, we tap into a profound state of awareness that allows us to experience the world—and ourselves—more deeply.

In this chapter, we'll explore how to embrace mindful presence and cultivate the ability to live a richer, more connected life. By learning to quiet the mind, not to silence it but to soften its grip, we open ourselves to the possibility of living in harmony with the world around us and within us.

The Overloaded Mind: When Thoughts Take Over

We've been conditioned to believe that thinking is the highest form of human intelligence. We analyze, we plan, we strategize, and in many ways, this has led to incredible achievements. But there's a price we pay when we allow thinking to become our default mode of interacting with the world. The mind, left unchecked, becomes a constant storyteller, creating dramas and anxieties that pull us away from the simplicity of being.

Imagine a day in your life where every moment is consumed by thought—what you need to do next, what someone said, how you should have acted differently. Each thought pulls you deeper into a spiral, and before you know it, the day has passed, but you've hardly lived in it. You've existed in your mind, consumed by the endless cycle of thinking, analyzing, and worrying.

Flourishing without thought doesn't mean that you stop thinking. It means that you stop letting thoughts dominate your existence. It means you learn how to step back, let thoughts come and go without grabbing hold of them, and allow yourself to simply experience the world without judgment or analysis.

What It Means to Flourish Without Thought

Flourishing without thought isn't the absence of intelligence or action. It's quite the opposite—it's the most profound way to engage with life. When you're no longer tethered to the constant barrage of mental noise, you become open to a more authentic way of experiencing the world.

Consider the difference between walking through a forest while worrying about an upcoming meeting versus walking through the same forest fully aware of the textures of the trees, the smell of the earth, and the rhythm of your footsteps. In the first scenario, you're physically present but mentally elsewhere. In the second, you're fully alive in the moment, experiencing life as it unfolds. This is flourishing without thought.

This isn't a passive state where you become detached from the world. Instead, it's an active form of engagement where your presence deepens. You see, hear, and feel more acutely because your mind isn't cluttered with unnecessary noise. You become more aware of subtle emotions, more connected to others, and more attuned to the present moment.

How to Cultivate Mindful Presence

Living with mindful presence is not something that happens overnight. It's a practice—a skill that requires patience and attention. The beauty of mindfulness is that it's accessible to everyone, no matter where you are or what you're doing. You don't need special tools or environments; you just need to bring your awareness to the present moment. Here's how you can begin to cultivate this mindful presence:

1. Tune Into Your Senses

Your senses are your greatest allies in the practice of mindful presence. When the mind starts to drift into overthinking, gently bring your attention back to your senses. Feel the ground beneath your feet, listen to the sounds around you, smell the air. Engage fully with what is happening in the moment. This sensory engagement helps anchor you in the present, breaking the cycle of overthinking.

For example, the next time you're eating, instead of rushing through the meal while thinking about your to-do list, pause. Taste each bite, notice the flavors, the textures, the warmth. When your mind starts to wander, gently bring it back to the experience of eating.

2. Let Thoughts Flow Without Grabbing Them

One of the key aspects of mindful presence is learning to observe your thoughts without getting caught up in them. This doesn't mean you push thoughts away or force yourself to stop thinking. Instead, imagine your thoughts as clouds passing across the sky. You don't need to chase them; just let them float by.

When a thought arises, acknowledge it without judgment and gently return your attention to the present moment. This practice of non-attachment to thoughts can be incredibly freeing, as it allows you to create space between yourself and the mental noise.

3. Breathe Into the Moment

Breathing is one of the simplest yet most powerful tools for grounding yourself in the present. When you focus on your breath, you give your mind a point of focus that naturally draws you into the present.

Whenever you feel overwhelmed by thoughts, take a few slow, deep breaths. Feel the air as it enters your lungs and notice how your body expands and contracts with each breath. This simple act of mindful breathing can create a sense of calm and clarity, allowing you to release the grip of overthinking and return to the present.

The Role of Stillness in a Busy World

We live in a world that prizes busyness. The more we do, the more we are often seen as successful or accomplished. But there's a hidden power in stillness, in stepping away from the constant doing and allowing ourselves to simply be. Stillness doesn't necessarily mean sitting in silence, although that can be part of it. It means cultivating a quiet mind, a mind that is free from the constant urge to plan, analyze, or judge.

Stillness is where creativity, insight, and peace arise. When the mind is still, it becomes clear, like a calm lake reflecting the sky. In this state of stillness, we can see things as they truly are, without the distortion of mental chatter.

Stillness doesn't mean inaction. In fact, the more still the mind, the more effective we become in our actions. When we're not distracted by unnecessary thoughts, we can engage with tasks, conversations, and challenges with greater focus and efficiency.

Letting Go of the Need for Control

One of the reasons we cling so tightly to thinking is that we believe it gives us control. If we can just think through every possibility, we imagine, we can avoid failure, pain, or uncertainty. But this belief is an illusion. Life is inherently uncertain, and no amount of thinking will change that.

Letting go of the need to control every outcome is one of the most liberating aspects of mindful presence. It allows us to surrender to the flow of life, trusting that we can handle whatever comes our way without needing to overthink every decision or scenario.

When we let go of control, we also let go of much of the stress and anxiety that come from trying to predict the future. We learn to respond to life as it unfolds, rather than constantly trying to force it into a predetermined mold.

Flourishing Through Simplicity

In a world that often equates success with complexity—more things, more achievements, more thoughts—there is a profound wisdom in simplicity. Flourishing without thought is closely linked to embracing simplicity, both in our external environment and in our inner life.

Simplicity doesn't mean deprivation; it means clarity. When we simplify, we strip away the unnecessary distractions and focus on what truly matters. This might mean decluttering our physical space, but more importantly, it means decluttering our minds. By letting go of the need to constantly think, plan, and worry, we make space for what is truly important—presence, connection, and peace.

When you simplify your life—whether it's your schedule, your belongings, or your thoughts—you create room to breathe, room to flourish. You become more open to the beauty of the present moment, more able to appreciate the richness of life that is often hidden beneath layers of mental and physical clutter.

Living a Life of Mindful Presence

Flourishing without thought is not a passive state. It is a vibrant, engaged way of being in the world. When we practice mindful presence, we don't become detached or indifferent; we become more deeply connected to life. We see things more clearly, feel emotions more deeply, and respond to situations with greater wisdom and compassion.

Living with mindful presence is an ongoing practice. It's not something we achieve once and for all, but something we cultivate every day, in every moment. It requires patience, kindness, and a willingness to return to the present whenever we find ourselves getting caught up in thought.

In the end, flourishing without thought is about reclaiming the joy and peace that are always available to us in the present moment. It's about stepping out of the mental noise and into the quiet, spacious awareness that allows us to fully experience life as it is—rich, complex, and beautifully imperfect.

The Gift of Presence

To flourish without thought is to discover a deeper, more meaningful way of living. It's about stepping out of the mental fog and into the clarity of the present moment. It's about letting go of the need for control and allowing ourselves to simply *be*—open, curious, and fully engaged with life.

As you continue on this journey, remember that mindful presence is not a destination but a practice. It's something you cultivate with each breath, each step, each moment of awareness. The more you practice, the more you will discover the quiet joy that comes from living in the here and now, free from the burden of overthinking and fully present in the beauty of life.

CHAPTER 9

REDEFINING AMBITION: ACHIEVING GOALS BEYOND THOUGHT

The New Ambition

Ambition has long been seen as a driving force behind success and achievement. Society often teaches us that the more we think, plan, strategize, and work toward our goals, the more likely we are to achieve them. We equate success with hard work, relentless focus, and mental discipline. But what if there's another way to achieve our goals—one that doesn't rely solely on the power of thought?

In this chapter, we'll explore the idea of **redefining ambition**—shifting our approach to goal-setting and achievement by integrating mindful presence. While thought is certainly important, there's a deeper, more intuitive way of working toward what we want in life, one that is grounded in awareness, flow, and alignment with the present moment. This new way of pursuing ambition doesn't discard thinking altogether, but it teaches us to balance thought with mindful action, allowing us to achieve goals more naturally and with less mental strain.

The key to this new ambition is learning to achieve goals beyond thought— by embracing presence, trusting intuition, and cultivating a sense of flow that allows us to navigate challenges with grace and ease. In the following sections, we'll redefine what it means to be ambitious and explore how we can achieve our goals while remaining grounded in mindful presence.

The Old Model of Ambition: Thinking and Hustling

Traditionally, ambition has been seen as a mental process. We set a goal, think of ways to achieve it, and then work tirelessly toward that goal until it's realized. This model emphasizes hustle—constant planning, strategizing, and pushing forward, often at the expense of our well-being and peace of mind.

This kind of ambition is driven by a sense of lack: we think we need to achieve something external to feel fulfilled, important, or successful. And while it's true that ambition can lead to achievements, it often comes with a cost. The relentless pursuit of goals can lead to stress, burnout, and dissatisfaction because the mind is always focused on what's next rather than appreciating what's happening now.

In this old model, success is measured by external markers—how much we've accomplished, how far we've advanced, or how much we've accumulated. But this model can feel exhausting and unsustainable, leaving little room for presence, joy, or connection with ourselves and others.

What if there's another way? What if ambition could be redefined to include the principles of mindfulness, where success isn't just about what we achieve but about how we feel and who we become in the process?

The Mindful Approach to Ambition

Redefining ambition doesn't mean letting go of our goals or settling for less. It means approaching our goals from a place of awareness, presence, and balance. Rather than pushing ourselves relentlessly toward achievement, we learn to move with the natural flow of life, aligning our actions with our values and inner wisdom. This approach is less about hustling and more about cultivating an inner sense of purpose and direction.

When we redefine ambition, we shift from a mindset of constant striving to one of mindful engagement. This involves trusting that when we are present and aligned with our deepest intentions, we are naturally guided toward the right actions, decisions, and opportunities. We stop trying to control every aspect of the journey and start working in harmony with the present moment.

This kind of ambition is both powerful and sustainable because it allows us to achieve our goals without depleting our energy or losing touch with ourselves. It's about achieving from a place of wholeness rather than from a sense of lack or need.

Flourishing in Flow: The Power of Intuitive Action

One of the most transformative aspects of achieving goals beyond thought is the concept of **flow**—a state where we are fully absorbed in what we're doing, and everything seems to come together effortlessly. In a state of flow, our actions become intuitive, our creativity is heightened, and we lose track of time as we become immersed in the present moment.

Flow is often described as the ultimate state of performance, where we tap into our highest potential without the strain of overthinking. It's a state where we are fully engaged, not because we're forcing ourselves to be, but because we are deeply connected to what we're doing.

Achieving goals from a state of flow is profoundly different from the hustle-oriented model of ambition. Instead of feeling overwhelmed or stressed, we feel energized and inspired. Our actions feel effortless, and we move toward our goals with a sense of ease rather than force.

Flow happens when we let go of the need to control everything and trust in our own intuition and abilities. It's a state that arises naturally when we are fully present, focused, and aligned with our purpose. In flow, we stop thinking about the goal and simply engage in the process, allowing the outcome to unfold naturally.

Letting Go of the Need for Constant Planning

One of the most challenging aspects of redefining ambition is letting go of the need for constant planning. We've been taught that success requires detailed plans, strict timelines, and precise steps. While planning has its place, it can also become a barrier to presence if we rely on it too heavily.

When we are overly attached to our plans, we lose flexibility and become stressed when things don't go according to schedule. We may become so focused on the steps we've laid out that we miss opportunities or insights that arise in the moment. In contrast, when we approach our goals with a sense of openness and adaptability, we allow room for creativity, intuition, and unexpected possibilities.

Instead of clinging to rigid plans, we can learn to create a broad vision of what we want to achieve, while remaining open to the natural unfolding of the journey. This requires trust—trust in ourselves, in the process, and in the idea that sometimes the path to success is not linear but dynamic and evolving.

When we let go of the need to control every detail, we create space for magic to happen. We allow ourselves to be guided by both our inner wisdom and the opportunities that life presents.

Balancing Intention with Surrender

At the heart of this new approach to ambition is the balance between intention and surrender. Intention is the clear, focused energy that drives us toward our goals. It's the force that gives direction and purpose to our actions. But intention alone is not enough. It must be balanced with surrender—the ability to let go of attachment to the outcome and trust the process.

Surrender doesn't mean giving up on our goals; it means releasing the need for everything to happen exactly as we envision. It means allowing life to unfold in its own time and trusting that things will work out as they are meant to, even if they don't follow our original plan.

By balancing intention with surrender, we achieve a state of flow where we are fully engaged with our goals but not weighed down by them. We take action, but we do so from a place of ease and trust, rather than from fear or control.

Achieving with Presence: The Joy of the Journey

One of the greatest shifts that occurs when we redefine ambition is that we begin to focus less on the outcome and more on the journey. Rather than being fixated on the end result, we find joy and fulfillment in the process of working toward our goals. This shift in focus allows us to stay present, savoring each step of the journey rather than rushing toward the finish line.

When we are fully present with our goals, we tap into a deeper sense of purpose and satisfaction. Every small step, every challenge, and every success becomes an opportunity for growth and learning. We stop measuring our worth by how much we achieve and start finding meaning in the way we engage with our work.

This presence-oriented approach to ambition also reduces the pressure we place on ourselves. When we focus on the process rather than the outcome, we give ourselves permission to make mistakes, learn from them, and adjust our course as needed. We become more resilient, more adaptable, and more open to the unexpected.

Creating Goals Aligned with Values

A key element of achieving goals beyond thought is ensuring that our goals are aligned with our deepest values. Often, we set goals based on external expectations or societal pressures, rather than from a place of authentic desire. When our goals are not aligned with our true values, we may achieve them, but they leave us feeling unfulfilled or disconnected.

Mindful ambition requires us to look inward and ask ourselves what truly matters. What are the values that guide our life? What kind of person do we want to become? When we set goals that are rooted in our values, they become more meaningful and fulfilling. We are no longer chasing external validation or success for its own sake. Instead, we are pursuing goals that resonate with who we are at our core.

Achieving goals aligned with our values brings a sense of purpose and direction that goes beyond material success. It connects us to something deeper, allowing us to flourish in a way that is both personal and profound.

Embracing Uncertainty and Trusting the Process

One of the greatest challenges in redefining ambition is learning to embrace uncertainty. In the traditional model of ambition, we often seek certainty and control. We want to know exactly how things will unfold and when we will achieve our goals. But life is unpredictable, and the path to success is rarely linear.

When we embrace mindful presence, we learn to navigate uncertainty with grace and confidence. We trust that even though we may not have all the answers, we are equipped to handle whatever comes our way. This trust allows us to move forward with less fear and more curiosity, knowing that each step of the journey brings new insights and opportunities.

Trusting the process means releasing the need for instant results and allowing our goals to evolve over time. It means recognizing that setbacks and challenges are not failures but part of the natural flow of life. When we stop resisting uncertainty and start embracing it, we open ourselves to greater possibilities and deeper growth.

Practical Steps for Achieving Goals Beyond Thought

Here are some practical steps to help you cultivate this new approach to ambition and achieve your goals with mindful presence:

- **Set Intentions, Not Just Goals**

When setting goals, focus on the intentions behind them. Ask yourself why you want to achieve a particular goal and how it aligns with your values. This will help you stay connected to the deeper meaning of your goals and prevent you from getting lost in the pursuit of external success.

- **Practice Mindful Action**

As you work toward your goals, practice being fully present in each step. Whether you're working on a project, having a conversation, or making a decision, bring your full attention to the task at hand. This will help you stay focused, reduce distractions, and cultivate a sense of flow in your work.

- **Cultivate Flexibility**

Allow yourself to be flexible with your plans. If things don't go as expected, adapt and adjust your approach. Trust that the detours and challenges along the way are part of the journey and that they often lead to new opportunities.

- **Celebrate the Process**

Rather than waiting until you've achieved your goal to feel satisfied, celebrate the small wins along the way. Acknowledge the progress you're making and take time to appreciate the growth and learning that happen throughout the journey.

Redefining Success on Your Own Terms

Redefining ambition is about more than achieving external goals; it's about finding a deeper sense of purpose, presence, and fulfillment in the process. By integrating mindful presence into your approach to ambition, you can achieve your goals with greater ease, clarity, and joy. You'll learn to trust the natural flow of life, embrace uncertainty, and stay aligned with your values as you move forward.

The path to success is not about constant striving or endless mental effort. It's about cultivating a sense of inner peace, allowing your intuition to guide you, and taking inspired action from a place of alignment and presence. When you redefine ambition in this way, you'll find that success becomes not just a destination but a way of being—a flourishing, joyful, and meaningful life lived in harmony with your true self.

CHAPTER 10

LOVE WITHOUT LIMITS UNCONDITIONAL CREATION

The Essence of Unconditional Creation

L ove has often been portrayed as an emotion, an attachment, or something exchanged between individuals. We fall in love, we earn love, or we lose it. However, at its core, love is something far more profound than an emotion—it is a state of being, an expansive and limitless energy that permeates all of life. This kind of love is not dependent on conditions, behaviors, or outcomes; it exists purely as a force of creation, an energy that shapes the world around us and within us.

In this chapter, we will explore the idea of **unconditional creation**, which is the act of bringing something into existence through love without limitation. Unconditional creation goes beyond the transactional nature of love that we often experience in relationships or society. It taps into the deeper, universal force of love that allows us to create, grow, and evolve from a place of abundance, acceptance, and boundless possibility.

We will discover how embracing this unconditional form of love can empower us to manifest our dreams, express ourselves authentically, and connect with others in ways that transcend expectations and conditions. By understanding the nature of love without limits, we can unlock our creative potential and learn to live in harmony with the world around us, creating without fear, restriction, or doubt.

The Nature of Conditional Love

Before we can understand unconditional love and its role in creation, it's important to recognize the limitations of conditional love. Conditional love is love that is based on specific terms, expectations, or circumstances. It's the kind of love that says, "I will love you if..." or "I can only love myself when..."

In relationships, conditional love is often transactional—meaning that it depends on whether certain needs or desires are met. We might love someone when they act in ways we approve of, but that love may waver when they fail to meet our expectations. Similarly, we may withhold love from ourselves if we feel that we haven't achieved enough, done enough, or been "good" enough.

Conditional love creates a world of limitation. It tells us that love must be earned, that we are not inherently worthy of love unless we meet certain criteria. This kind of love stifles our creative energy because it keeps us trapped in fear— fear of rejection, failure, or inadequacy.

When we operate from conditional love, we become constrained by self-judgment, anxiety, and perfectionism. We fear stepping outside of the boxes we or others have created, and as a result, we limit our potential to create and experience life in its fullest expression.

Unconditional Creation: Love as a Creative Force

Unconditional creation is rooted in the understanding that love is not something we have to earn or deserve; it is something we already possess. It is the very fabric of our being. This kind of love is limitless, infinite, and always available to us. When we embrace unconditional love, we step into the role of co-creators with the universe, bringing our unique expressions of life into existence without fear or hesitation.

To create unconditionally means to tap into the love that flows freely from within us, unburdened by expectations or judgments. This kind of creation doesn't come from a place of striving, perfectionism, or the need to prove ourselves. Instead, it arises naturally and effortlessly, like a river flowing toward the sea. When we create from a place of unconditional love, we are not concerned with outcomes or validation; we are simply expressing the fullness of who we are.

Think of unconditional creation as the act of painting on a blank canvas without worrying about whether the painting will be good or bad. You are creating for the sake of creation itself, allowing the act of creation to be a reflection of the love and energy within you. There is no fear of making mistakes, no need to control or perfect the process. You simply allow yourself to create with abandon, knowing that what you are bringing into existence is valuable and beautiful because it comes from an authentic place.

The Relationship Between Love and Creation

Love and creation are inextricably linked. To love is to create, and to create is to love. Every act of creation—whether it's art, writing, a relationship, a business, or a moment of kindness—comes from a place of love. When we create, we are expressing the love we feel for life, for ourselves, and for others.

In moments of true creation, there is no separation between the creator and the creation. There is a flow, a unity, in which love is expressed through the act of bringing something new into the world. This is the essence of unconditional creation—creating not for recognition or approval but for the joy of the process, for the love that moves through us and becomes manifest in the world.

When we allow ourselves to create without limits, we transcend the boundaries that often keep us stuck. We stop worrying about whether we are good enough, talented enough, or worthy enough. We simply create because we are filled with love for the act of creation itself. This is how we become co-creators with the universe, tapping into the infinite well of possibilities that exist within us.

Letting Go of Perfectionism and Control

One of the greatest obstacles to unconditional creation is the desire for perfection and control. We often place conditions on our creativity, believing that what we create must meet certain standards in order to be valuable. We might think, "If I can't do it perfectly, why do it at all?" This kind of thinking stifles our ability to create freely and joyfully.

Perfectionism is rooted in fear—fear of failure, fear of judgment, fear of not being enough. But unconditional creation is the opposite of fear. It is the act of letting go of the need for control and allowing love to guide the creative process. When we let go of perfectionism, we open ourselves to the possibility of creating something raw, authentic, and beautiful, even if it doesn't meet the standards we've been taught to value.

Letting go of control means trusting the process of creation, knowing that what we create doesn't have to be flawless to be meaningful. It means embracing the imperfections, the messiness, and the unpredictability of creation as part of the journey. When we release the need for everything to be perfect, we free ourselves to create with more courage, spontaneity, and joy.

Creating from a Place of Wholeness

Unconditional creation arises when we recognize that we are already whole. We do not need to achieve, produce, or create something spectacular to prove our worth. Our worthiness is inherent. When we create from a place of wholeness, we are no longer driven by the need to fill a void or gain approval. Instead, we create as an expression of the love and completeness we already possess.

This shift in perspective is transformative. When we stop creating from a place of lack or insecurity, our creations become more aligned with our true selves. We stop comparing ourselves to others or worrying about how our creations will be received. Instead, we focus on the act of creation itself, allowing it to be a reflection of the love and wholeness within us.

Creating from wholeness also means recognizing that our creations are extensions of ourselves, but they do not define us. Whether a project is successful or not, whether our work is praised or criticized, it does not diminish our inherent worth. When we create from a place of love, we are free to experiment, take risks, and explore new possibilities without fear of failure or rejection.

The Freedom of Unconditional Creation

Unconditional creation offers a profound sense of freedom. When we release the need for external validation, approval, or recognition, we are free to create in ways that are authentic and true to ourselves. We are no longer bound by the expectations of others or the limitations we place on ourselves.

This freedom allows us to explore new ideas, try new things, and take creative risks without fear of judgment. It opens the door to greater innovation, creativity, and self-expression. When we create without limits, we tap into a wellspring of inspiration that is always available to us. We become conduits for the flow of love and creativity that exists within us and all around us.

Unconditional creation also allows us to embrace the unknown. We don't need to have all the answers or know exactly how something will turn out. We trust the process of creation, knowing that the act of creating is valuable in itself, regardless of the outcome. This trust allows us to move forward with confidence, even when the path is uncertain.

Living a Life of Unconditional Creation

To live a life of unconditional creation is to live in alignment with love. It means embracing the creative energy that flows through you and allowing it to guide your actions, decisions, and expressions. It means trusting that what you create is valuable, not because of how it is received by others, but because it is an authentic expression of who you are.

Unconditional creation is not limited to traditional forms of creativity like art or writing. It applies to every area of life—relationships, work, personal growth, and even everyday interactions. Every moment offers an opportunity to create from a place of love, whether it's through a kind word, a thoughtful gesture, or a new idea.

When we live a life of unconditional creation, we are constantly in a state of expansion. We are not limited by fear, doubt, or the need for approval. Instead, we are guided by the love that flows through us, allowing us to create a life that is rich, meaningful, and aligned with our true selves.

Practical Steps for Embracing Unconditional Creation

Here are some practical steps to help you cultivate the mindset of unconditional creation:

1. Create Without Expectations

Engage in creative activities without setting expectations for the outcome. Whether it's painting, writing, cooking, or another form of expression, allow yourself to create purely for the joy of it, without worrying about whether it's "good" or "perfect."

2. Practice Self-Compassion

When self-doubt or perfectionism arises, practice self-compassion. Remind yourself that you are already worthy, and that your creations are valuable simply because they come from you. Let go of harsh judgments and embrace the process of learning and growth.

3. Focus on the Process, Not the Result

Shift your focus from the result of your creative efforts to the process itself. Enjoy the act of creating, and trust that the outcome will take care of itself. When you are fully present in the process, you create with more ease and authenticity.

4. Explore New Forms of Creation

Step outside of your comfort zone and try new forms of creation. Whether it's a new hobby, a different way of expressing yourself, or an innovative idea, allow yourself to explore without fear of failure. The more you experiment, the more you expand your creative potential.

Conclusion: Love as the Ultimate Creative Force

Unconditional creation is a way of living that is grounded in love—love for ourselves, love for the act of creation, and love for the world around us. When we embrace this limitless love, we open ourselves to the infinite possibilities that exist within us. We become co-creators with the universe, bringing our unique gifts and expressions into the world in ways that are authentic, meaningful, and aligned with our true nature.

As you continue on this journey of unconditional creation, remember that your worth is not defined by what you produce or achieve. You are already whole, and your creative potential is boundless. Trust in the love that flows through you, and allow it to guide your actions, your expressions, and your life.

CHAPTER 11

LIVING FULFILLED
WHAT COMES AFTER PEACE AND JOY?

Beyond the Quest for Peace and Joy

We often think of peace and joy as the ultimate goals in life. Many of us spend years—if not our entire lives—seeking these two elusive experiences, believing that once we attain them, we will have reached the pinnacle of fulfillment. Peace brings relief from the chaos of our minds, and joy lifts our spirits, reminding us that life can be beautiful. But what if peace and joy are not the final destination? What if, after achieving them, there is another level of living, a state of being that goes beyond what we typically associate with fulfillment?

In this chapter, we explore the question: *What comes after peace and joy?* While these states are essential and enriching, they are not the end of the road. Once we cultivate them, we are invited to enter a new dimension of living—a state of deep fulfillment where purpose, connection, and meaning become the foundation of our existence. Living fulfilled is not about resting in peace and joy alone; it's about using those states as a springboard to engage with life more profoundly, tapping into our highest potential and contributing to the world in meaningful ways.

The Threshold: Arriving at Peace and Joy

Before we dive into what lies beyond peace and joy, it's important to recognize the significance of these experiences in our lives. Peace is the antidote to the turmoil of overthinking, anxiety, and the mental clutter that often dominates our minds. It is the stillness we seek when life feels chaotic, a state of being where we are no longer pulled by the external demands or internal fears that typically drive us.

Joy, on the other hand, is the lightness of being, the natural expression of our true selves when we are free from the weight of worry and self-doubt. It is the pure happiness that arises when we are fully present, connected to ourselves, and aligned with the flow of life.

Reaching a state of peace and joy is a profound achievement. It often requires years of inner work, mindfulness, meditation, and self-reflection. But what happens after we find peace? Do we simply sit in our joy, content to be in the moment forever, or is there more to explore?

This is where the journey toward fulfillment begins—when peace and joy become the foundation, not the endpoint, of our lives.

The Emergence of Purpose: Living with Meaning

Once we have cultivated peace and joy within ourselves, we often begin to ask deeper questions about our place in the world. We realize that while these states bring personal happiness, there is a desire for something more—a longing for purpose and meaning. This is the first step beyond peace and joy: discovering how to live a life that feels purposeful.

Purpose is not something we achieve by chance. It is something we uncover through reflection, experience, and engagement with the world around us. It goes beyond the self; it is about contributing to something larger than ourselves. Purpose is what gives our actions weight and significance. It is what drives us to wake up each morning with a sense of motivation, knowing that we are part of something meaningful.

When we align our lives with a purpose that resonates deeply with us, we move beyond seeking personal peace and joy and step into a life of service, creativity, and impact. This is where true fulfillment begins—not in the passive enjoyment of peaceful moments but in the active pursuit of living in harmony with our highest values.

The Call to Contribution

One of the greatest realizations that comes after finding peace and joy is the desire to contribute. When we are no longer preoccupied with our own suffering or inner conflicts, we are free to look outward, to see where our unique gifts, talents, and passions can make a difference in the lives of others.

Contribution doesn't have to be grandiose. It can be as simple as offering kindness to those around us, using our creativity to inspire others, or dedicating time to causes that align with our values. The key is that our actions come from a place of abundance, not from a sense of obligation or expectation.

In Zen philosophy, there is the concept of **dana**—the practice of giving without expecting anything in return. Dana is an expression of generosity that arises naturally when we are at peace with ourselves and no longer driven by the need for external validation. It is the realization that true fulfillment comes not from accumulating more but from giving what we have to others.

Living fulfilled means recognizing that our contributions, no matter how small, have the power to ripple out and create positive change in the world. It is about understanding that we are interconnected and that our well-being is deeply tied to the well-being of others.

Connecting with Others: Relationships Beyond the Self

As we move beyond the quest for personal peace and joy, we begin to see the importance of our relationships with others. Human connection is one of the most profound sources of fulfillment, yet it is often neglected in our pursuit of individual happiness. Once we find peace within ourselves, we are better equipped to form deep, authentic connections with others, free from the baggage of insecurity, fear, or ego.

True connection requires vulnerability—the willingness to be seen and to see others as they are, without judgment or pretense. It means engaging with others from a place of love, acceptance, and presence, rather than from a place of need or expectation.

When we live in a state of fulfillment, we are no longer looking for others to complete us or fill the gaps in our lives. Instead, our relationships become a space where we can share our fullness, offering support, understanding, and love without the need for reciprocity.

In these relationships, we experience a deeper sense of joy and peace, not because we are seeking them but because they arise naturally from the connection itself. This is one of the great gifts of living fulfilled: the ability to engage in relationships that are nourishing, expansive, and free from the constraints of conditional love.

Creativity and Expression: Expanding Through Creation

Living fulfilled also opens the door to a deeper level of creativity and self-expression. When we are no longer consumed by the search for personal happiness or peace, we have the freedom to explore our creative potential without the limitations of self-doubt or fear of failure.

Creativity, in this context, is not limited to the arts. It is the act of bringing something new into the world—whether that be ideas, solutions, projects, or relationships. Creativity is an essential part of living fulfilled because it allows us to engage with life actively, contributing to the ongoing evolution of the world around us.

This level of creativity is different from the kind of creativity that is driven by ego or the need for recognition. It is an expression of our true selves, a reflection of the inner peace and joy we have cultivated, and it comes from a place of abundance rather than lack.

When we create from a place of fulfillment, we are not attached to the outcome. We create for the sake of creation itself, knowing that the act of expressing ourselves is valuable, regardless of how it is received. This is the ultimate form of freedom in creativity—the ability to engage fully with the process, without the need for external validation or approval.

The Role of Inner Stillness: Thriving in the Present

Even as we move beyond peace and joy, the practice of inner stillness remains an essential part of living fulfilled. Inner stillness is the foundation upon which all other aspects of fulfillment are built. It is the quiet space within us that allows us to navigate the complexities of life with grace and clarity.

In a world that is constantly moving and changing, inner stillness provides a sense of grounding. It allows us to stay connected to ourselves, even as we engage with the world around us. Through mindfulness, meditation, and other practices that cultivate stillness, we maintain our connection to the present moment, ensuring that we are living in alignment with our values and intentions.

Inner stillness is not a state of inaction. It is a state of awareness that allows us to move through life with intention and presence. It is the space from which we can respond to life's challenges, rather than reacting to them from a place of fear or anxiety.

When we live fulfilled, we cultivate this inner stillness as a daily practice, knowing that it is the key to maintaining peace and joy even as we pursue our goals, engage with others, and contribute to the world.

Living in Alignment: Walking the Path of Integrity

71

Another essential aspect of living fulfilled is living in alignment with our values and our true selves. When we live in alignment, there is no disconnect between what we believe and how we act. Our thoughts, words, and actions are congruent, and we feel a deep sense of integrity in everything we do.

Living in alignment requires self-awareness and honesty. It means continually checking in with ourselves to ensure that we are making choices that reflect our highest values and intentions. When we live out of alignment—when we make decisions based on fear, ego, or societal pressures—we feel a sense of disconnection and unease. But when we live in alignment, we experience a deep sense of peace and fulfillment because we know that we are living authentically.

Alignment also means honoring our boundaries and taking care of ourselves. It is not about sacrificing our well-being for the sake of others or for the pursuit of external success. Instead, it is about finding balance—honoring both our inner needs and our outer commitments.

Beyond the Self: Finding Fulfillment in Service

Once we have cultivated peace and joy, and once we have aligned our lives with our purpose, something remarkable happens: we begin to experience fulfillment through service. This doesn't mean that we lose ourselves in the needs of others, but rather that we find deeper meaning by contributing to the well-being of those around us.

Service can take many forms. It can be as simple as offering kindness and support to those in our immediate circle, or as grand as dedicating our lives to a cause that aligns with our values. The key is that we engage in service from a place of love and abundance, rather than from a sense of obligation or martyrdom.

When we serve others, we are reminded of our interconnectedness. We see that our well-being is tied to the well-being of those around us, and we experience a deeper sense of purpose in knowing that our actions have a positive impact on the world.

This is one of the most profound forms of fulfillment—knowing that we are contributing to something larger than ourselves, that our lives have meaning beyond our individual experiences, and that we are leaving the world a little better than we found it.

Evolving Beyond Fulfillment: The Path of Continuous Growth

Even as we reach a state of fulfillment, life continues to evolve, and so do we. Living fulfilled does not mean that we have reached a static endpoint. It means that we are continually growing, learning, and expanding in new ways.

The beauty of living fulfilled is that it is not a destination but a journey. As we deepen our understanding of ourselves and the world, we discover new layers of meaning and purpose. We continue to evolve, both internally and externally, finding new ways to express ourselves, contribute to the world, and live in alignment with our values.

This continuous growth is what makes life rich and dynamic. It ensures that even as we experience fulfillment, there is always more to explore, more to create, and more to learn.

Practical Steps for Living Fulfilled

Here are some practical steps to help you cultivate a life of fulfillment beyond peace and joy:

- **Reflect on Your Purpose**

Take time to reflect on your purpose in life. What are the values that guide you? What brings you a sense of meaning and fulfillment? Use these reflections to align your actions with your purpose.

- **Practice Generosity**

Engage in acts of generosity and service. Whether it's offering your time, skills, or resources, find ways to contribute to the well-being of others. Remember that true generosity comes from a place of love, not obligation.

- **Cultivate Authentic Relationships**

Invest in deep, authentic relationships that nourish your soul. Be present, be vulnerable, and be willing to engage with others in meaningful ways.

- **Embrace Creativity**

Explore new forms of creativity and self-expression. Allow yourself to create without fear of judgment or failure. Remember that creativity is a reflection of your inner joy and fulfillment.

73

- **Maintain Inner Stillness**

Continue to cultivate inner stillness through mindfulness, meditation, or other practices. This will help you stay grounded and present, even as you pursue your goals and engage with the world.

A Life Beyond Peace and Joy

Living fulfilled is a state of being that transcends personal peace and joy. It is a life of purpose, contribution, connection, and continuous growth. It is about finding meaning not just in what we achieve but in how we live, how we engage with others, and how we contribute to the world around us.

As you move beyond the quest for peace and joy, embrace the opportunities for deeper fulfillment that arise. Live in alignment with your values, connect with others from a place of love, and use your unique gifts to make a positive impact on the world. In doing so, you will discover that true fulfillment is not a destination but a way of living—a life that is rich, meaningful, and full of endless possibilities.

CHAPTER 12

THE ILLUSION OF JUDGMENT NOTHING IS GOOD OR BAD

Stepping Beyond Judgment

Life is full of labels. We categorize moments, people, and experiences into tidy boxes—good or bad, right or wrong, success or failure. This habit of judgment forms the bedrock of how we navigate the world, but it also quietly limits us. We paint our reality with judgments, distorting the complexity of life into simple, binary classifications. But what if this act of judging is an illusion? What if life isn't actually as black and white as we make it out to be? What if nothing is inherently good or bad?

In this chapter, we'll explore the profound freedom that comes from releasing the need to judge everything. By moving beyond this binary thinking, we open ourselves to a life of richer experiences, deeper connection, and greater peace. Without judgment clouding our perceptions, we begin to see the world as it truly is—fluid, evolving, and full of possibilities. We'll delve into how to shed the habit of constant categorization and embrace a mindset that sees beyond labels, where experiences simply exist as they are.

The Mental Reflex of Judgment

Judgment has become second nature to many of us, a reflexive response we hardly even notice. It's deeply ingrained, woven into our daily experiences. We evaluate the weather, rate our performance at work, or size up our interactions with others. We do this because it feels like a way to gain control, to bring order to a seemingly chaotic world. When we label something as "good" or "bad," we believe we're defining it, giving it clarity.

But in reality, these judgments are more like a fog—obscuring the true nature of things. We think we're seeing clearly when we label something as "wrong" or "unfortunate," but what we're often doing is reducing the complexity of that situation to a simplistic interpretation. This simplification limits us, locking us into fixed viewpoints that prevent us from seeing the broader picture.

Judgment makes us think we are in control, that we understand the world around us. Yet, the more we judge, the less we actually see. We miss the nuances, the subtle layers of experience that cannot be captured in rigid categories. Life is far too intricate, too dynamic, to be boxed into these mental categories.

The Subtle Art of Observation Without Judgment

Imagine walking through a forest. You hear birds, feel the breeze, and notice the rustling of leaves. Without labeling any of these sensations as "good" or "bad," you simply take it all in. This pure observation is something we can practice, yet it goes against the grain of how we've been taught to navigate life. Our minds are trained to evaluate: "This tree is beautiful," "That sound is too loud," or "It's too hot today."

But when we remove judgment from the equation, we open ourselves up to experiencing the moment in its fullness. No longer are we confined to preconceived labels or categories. The tree is no longer just "beautiful"; it's alive, it's old, it's thriving in its unique way. The sound isn't "too loud"; it just is. And in that observation, free from judgment, we discover a deeper connection with the world around us.

This shift from judgment to observation can be life-changing. It allows us to meet each moment without preconceived ideas, welcoming it for what it is, not what we think it should be. This doesn't mean we stop discerning or making choices, but it does mean we stop coloring our experiences with a constant stream of judgment.

Why We Judge: The Illusion of Certainty

Judgment gives us a false sense of certainty. We cling to it because it makes us feel like we understand the world. By categorizing things as "good" or "bad," we feel grounded, as though we have a firm grasp on what's happening. But this is where judgment misleads us. The world is inherently uncertain, and no amount of mental labeling can change that.

When we label a situation, we close off other interpretations and possibilities. A setback at work, for example, might initially feel like a failure. If we judge it as such, we become trapped in that narrative. But if we allow it to simply be—a situation without a fixed label—we create space to learn, grow, and see new opportunities that might arise from it.

Judgment makes us feel safe in a world that's unpredictable, but in doing so, it narrows our vision. By releasing the need to judge, we don't fall into chaos; instead, we find a deeper sense of clarity, one that embraces uncertainty and thrives in its openness.

The Paradox of Good and Bad

Consider this paradox: what seems bad today might lead to something positive tomorrow. Likewise, what feels good now could bring unexpected challenges later. Life constantly shifts and evolves, yet when we judge something as definitively good or bad, we freeze it in time. We fixate on a moment, assuming that our judgment is the final word, when in reality, everything is in flux.

Think about the challenges you've faced in the past. How often has something that seemed negative at the time later revealed itself as an opportunity for growth, change, or even transformation? Conversely, moments that felt perfect may have led to unexpected difficulties. The point is that life isn't static. When we stop trying to pin experiences down with rigid labels, we allow them to unfold in their full complexity.

By stepping away from the binary framework of good and bad, we open ourselves to the true nature of life—one that is rich, layered, and constantly evolving. Every experience has the potential to teach us something valuable, but only if we stop locking it into a pre-determined box.

The Practice of Letting Go of Judgment

So, how do we begin to release judgment? It starts with awareness. The next time you find yourself labeling a situation, a person, or yourself, pause. Notice the judgment as it arises. You don't need to fight it or suppress it. Simply acknowledge it and ask yourself: *What am I really seeing here? Is this judgment limiting my understanding?*

As you practice noticing your judgments, you'll begin to see them as just thoughts—constructs of the mind, not absolute truths. This awareness alone can begin to dissolve the power that judgment holds over you. Instead of reacting to the world through a lens of good and bad, you start to experience it as it is: a flowing, ever-changing reality that cannot be fully captured by labels.

Letting go of judgment doesn't mean we stop making decisions or exercising

77

discernment. It means we stop clinging to rigid definitions that prevent us from seeing clearly. With time, this practice of releasing judgment becomes second nature, allowing us to live with greater openness and curiosity.

The Freedom of Non-Judgment

When we release the need to judge everything, a remarkable freedom emerges. No longer bound by the mental cages we create, we start to live with a greater sense of ease. Life becomes less about managing our expectations and more about experiencing the world with fresh eyes. The pressure to constantly assess and evaluate falls away, and we discover a more fluid way of being.

In relationships, this shift can be transformative. Instead of judging others based on preconceived ideas or past experiences, we begin to meet them where they are. We see people not through the lens of our judgments, but through the lens of compassion and understanding. This doesn't mean we ignore harmful behavior or let go of boundaries, but it does mean that we approach others with more empathy, recognizing that everyone is on their own path, just as we are.

In our personal lives, releasing judgment allows us to cultivate a more loving relationship with ourselves. Instead of constantly evaluating our worth or critiquing our actions, we learn to accept ourselves as we are, flaws and all. This self-acceptance creates the foundation for true growth, because we're no longer trying to live up to impossible standards or punishing ourselves for perceived failures.

A Life Without Labels: Embracing the Present Moment

When we let go of judgment, we open ourselves to the present moment in a way that few people ever experience. Life becomes richer, more vivid, and more meaningful. We stop seeing the world as a series of events to be labeled and evaluated, and instead, we experience it as an unfolding process, one that is full of surprises, challenges, and beauty.

Without judgment, we find that the present moment is enough. We no longer need to compare it to some ideal version of reality, nor do we need to measure it against past experiences or future expectations. The present moment, free from the burden of judgment, becomes a place of peace and clarity.

This is the true gift of living without judgment: the ability to be fully present with life as it is, without constantly needing to reshape it to fit our mental constructs. In this space of non-judgment, we find a deeper connection to ourselves, to others, and to the world around us.

Embracing Life's Complexity

In the end, the illusion of judgment is just that—an illusion. It tricks us into thinking that we understand the world when, in reality, we're only seeing a fraction of its complexity. By letting go of judgment, we open ourselves to a richer, fuller experience of life, one that transcends the simplistic labels of good and bad.

Life is complex, messy, and ever-changing. When we release the need to categorize everything, we find that this complexity is not something to be feared, but something to be embraced. The more we let go of judgment, the more we can appreciate the vastness of life, with all its contradictions and surprises.

Practical Steps to Live Without Judgment

Here are a few ways you can begin practicing non-judgment in your everyday life:

- **Notice Your Judgments**

Throughout the day, take note of when you're judging something—whether it's a situation, a person, or yourself. Simply becoming aware of your judgments is the first step toward releasing them.

- **Practice Curiosity**

When you catch yourself judging, try shifting to curiosity. Instead of labeling something as good or bad, ask yourself: *What can I learn from this? What else might be true here?*

- **Engage in Non-Judgmental Observation**

Spend time observing your surroundings, your thoughts, and your emotions without labeling them. Let them exist without needing to categorize them as positive or negative.

- **Cultivate Compassion**

When judgment arises, respond with compassion. Remind yourself that everyone—including you—is doing the best they can, and that judgment often clouds our ability to see the full picture.

Living Beyond Judgment

By letting go of the illusion of judgment, we unlock a new way of experiencing the world. We move beyond the binary framework of good and bad, embracing the complexity, fluidity, and beauty of life as it is. In this space of non-judgment, we find freedom, clarity, and deeper connection—to ourselves, to others, and to the world around us.

Living beyond judgment isn't about becoming indifferent or passive. It's about seeing life with fresh eyes, experiencing the present moment fully, and engaging with the world from a place of openness and curiosity. As we release the need to categorize and control, we discover a deeper, more authentic way of being—one that invites us to live with greater peace, compassion, and understanding.

CHAPTER 13

TRUSTING INTUITION: ACTING WITHOUT MENTAL INTERFERENCE

The Power of Intuition in a Noisy World

In the world we live in today, we are constantly bombarded with information. From the moment we wake up, our phones, computers, and conversations flood us with opinions, facts, and advice on how we should live our lives, make decisions, and plan our futures. It can be overwhelming. We rely on logic, reason, and external input to make sense of it all, hoping that this will lead us to clarity. But there is a deeper source of wisdom that lies within each of us, often drowned out by the noise—**intuition**.

Intuition is that subtle, almost instinctive knowing that comes without the need for conscious reasoning. It's the feeling you get when something just doesn't sit right, or when you know in your gut that you should take a certain action, even if you can't explain why. Intuition is a powerful guide, but in a world that emphasizes thinking over feeling, many of us struggle to trust it.

This chapter delves into the practice of trusting intuition, teaching you how to recognize, develop, and act on it without the constant interference of your mind. We will explore how intuition differs from logic, how to overcome the mental barriers that prevent us from trusting it, and why intuition is a critical element in achieving a life that is both meaningful and fulfilling.

What Is Intuition? An Unseen, Unspoken Knowing

Intuition is often described as a "gut feeling," but it goes beyond that. It's an immediate, unconscious form of knowing that doesn't follow a clear, linear path like rational thought. Unlike logic, which operates by analyzing, comparing, and calculating, intuition presents itself as a whole. It's instantaneous, not requiring us to work through each piece of information step-by-step.

It's important to understand that intuition isn't some mystical force. It arises from a deep well of internal knowledge—our experiences, memories, and even the unconscious patterns we've observed throughout our lives. While logic processes information linearly, intuition draws from a vast, interconnected network of past learnings, senses, and emotional intelligence to form a picture instantly.

For instance, imagine you meet someone for the first time. Something about their demeanor gives you a sense of unease, even though they haven't said or done anything explicitly negative. You may not be able to explain it, but your intuition is picking up on subtle cues, body language, or tone of voice that signal caution. Your mind might tell you to ignore it, but this gut feeling is real and often worth exploring.

The Difference Between Intuition and Instinct

While intuition is often described as a "gut feeling," it's important to distinguish it from instinct. Instinct is a primal, biological response. It's the hardwired behavior that kicks in during life-or-death situations. For example, the fight-or-flight response when faced with danger is instinct. You don't think about running when you see a predator—you just run.

Intuition, on the other hand, is more refined. It is not simply a survival mechanism but a nuanced form of wisdom that comes from within. Intuition arises from the integration of mind, body, and spirit, drawing on everything we've learned—consciously or unconsciously—about the world around us. It connects us to deeper layers of understanding that transcend logical thought and analysis.

In modern life, we don't often face immediate physical danger, but we are constantly faced with decisions—big and small—that affect our emotional, psychological, and spiritual well-being. This is where intuition comes into play. It helps guide us through the complexity of life, pointing us toward decisions that are aligned with our deepest truths, even when we can't rationally explain why.

Why We Struggle to Trust Intuition: The Overactive Mind

The challenge with trusting intuition isn't that it doesn't exist; it's that our minds are conditioned to override it. From a young age, we are taught to value logic, reason, and measurable evidence over feelings or inner knowing. We're taught to seek advice, research options, and gather as much information as possible before making a decision.

While this can be helpful, it often leads to overthinking. The mind can become so bogged down with conflicting information, fear of making the wrong choice, or societal pressures that it drowns out the voice of intuition. Instead of acting from a place of inner knowing, we become stuck in analysis paralysis, second-guessing ourselves and doubting the subtle messages our intuition is trying to send.

This mental interference is like static in a radio signal. The more we overthink, the more we obscure the clarity of our intuitive voice. To trust intuition, we need to quiet the mind, learn to recognize when it's getting in the way, and practice letting go of the need for absolute certainty in favor of trusting our deeper inner wisdom.

How to Recognize Intuition: Subtle, Yet Powerful Signals

One of the first steps in learning to trust intuition is recognizing it. For many people, intuition doesn't shout—it whispers. It's easy to miss or dismiss because it doesn't present itself in the same way as logical thought. It's not always a clear thought or a fully formed idea; instead, it's a feeling, a sensation, or a sense of knowing that arises spontaneously.

Intuition often feels like a sudden insight or a flash of clarity. You might be grappling with a difficult decision, unsure of which direction to take, and then— out of nowhere—the answer seems to arrive fully formed. It might feel like a quiet nudge or a sense of peace around a certain choice, even if that choice doesn't seem rational on the surface.

The body is also a powerful indicator of intuition. You may notice physical sensations when intuition speaks—such as a tightening in the chest when something feels off, or a sense of lightness when you are on the right path. The body and mind are deeply connected, and intuition often communicates through physical signals that bypass logical thought.

Zen and Intuition: A Path to Simplicity

In Zen philosophy, intuition is closely linked to the concept of **satori**, a sudden awakening or enlightenment that occurs when the mind becomes still and clear. Zen practitioners emphasize the importance of being fully present in the moment, free from the distractions of past or future concerns. In this state of mindfulness, intuition can arise naturally because the mind is not cluttered with overthinking.

Zen encourages us to let go of mental interference and trust in the flow of life. When we stop trying to control everything through logic and analysis, we open ourselves up to the deeper wisdom that intuition provides. By quieting the constant chatter of the mind, we create space for intuitive insights to emerge effortlessly, without needing to be forced or figured out.

As Zen teachings suggest, intuition often arises in moments of stillness—when we are not actively searching for answers, but simply allowing them to come to us. In this way, intuition is a natural extension of mindfulness, born from the ability to stay present and aware without judgment or mental noise.

The Role of Trust: Acting on Intuition Without Fear

Once we recognize intuition, the next challenge is learning to trust it. This can be difficult, especially when intuition leads us in a direction that contradicts logic or goes against what others expect from us. Trusting intuition requires courage because it often involves stepping into the unknown, making choices that can't be easily explained or justified by reason alone.

One of the greatest barriers to trusting intuition is fear—fear of making the wrong decision, fear of failure, or fear of judgment from others. The mind craves certainty and safety, and when intuition pushes us toward a path that feels risky or unconventional, the mind tries to intervene, pulling us back into overthinking.

But the beauty of intuition is that it comes from a place of deep inner alignment. When we act on intuition, we are acting in accordance with our true selves. Even if the outcome isn't what we expected, intuition leads us toward growth, learning, and experiences that are ultimately in alignment with our higher purpose.

To cultivate trust in intuition, start with small steps. Instead of trying to overhaul your entire life based on an intuitive hunch, begin by following your intuition in smaller decisions. Over time, as you see how intuition guides you, your confidence in it will grow. Trust builds with practice, and the more you act on your intuitive sense, the more you'll discover how reliable it truly is.

Overcoming the Mind's Resistance: Letting Go of Overthinking

Overthinking is one of the biggest obstacles to trusting intuition. The mind has a natural tendency to seek out every possible outcome, to weigh the pros and cons, and to predict what might happen if we choose one path over another. While this analytical approach can be useful in certain situations, it often leads to confusion and doubt when we're dealing with more complex or emotional decisions.

To overcome overthinking, it's essential to recognize when the mind is taking over. Ask yourself: *Am I analyzing this situation to the point of paralysis? Am I trying to control an outcome that is uncertain by thinking through every possible scenario?* If the answer is yes, it may be time to step back, take a deep breath, and tune into what your intuition is telling you.

One way to break free from overthinking is to engage in practices that help quiet the mind, such as meditation, yoga, or deep breathing exercises. These practices create space for intuition to rise to the surface, free from the mental clutter that often drowns it out. When the mind is calm, intuition has a chance to speak clearly.

The Difference Between Fear and Intuition

It's important to distinguish between fear and intuition, as they can sometimes feel similar. Fear often masquerades as intuition, leading us to believe that we should avoid certain situations or decisions because they make us uncomfortable. But fear is driven by past experiences, limiting beliefs, and a desire to stay safe, while intuition is driven by inner wisdom.

One way to tell the difference between fear and intuition is to notice the quality of the feeling. Fear often feels heavy, constricting, or anxious, while intuition feels calm, clear, and steady. Intuition doesn't come with the emotional charge that fear carries; it's more of a quiet knowing that feels grounded and aligned.

Another key difference is that fear is often rooted in the mind's need to control, while intuition is connected to trust. Fear tries to protect us from the unknown, while intuition encourages us to step into the unknown with confidence. By tuning into the body and the emotional tone of the feeling, you can begin to discern whether you're being guided by fear or by your intuitive wisdom.

The Intersection of Intuition and Creativity

Creativity and intuition are deeply intertwined. Both arise from a place beyond logical thought, drawing from a reservoir of inspiration that is often difficult to explain. Artists, writers, musicians, and innovators frequently speak of moments when ideas or solutions seem to come out of nowhere—this is intuition at work.

When we engage in creative activities, we naturally tap into our intuition. We stop thinking in rigid, linear ways and allow ourselves to explore, experiment, and play. This creative flow is very much like the intuitive flow that guides us through life. The more we practice creativity, the more we strengthen our connection to intuition.

To cultivate intuition, consider engaging in activities that encourage creative thinking—whether that's painting, writing, dancing, or simply brainstorming without judgment. Creativity opens the door to intuitive insights, helping us break free from the limitations of logical thought and tap into deeper levels of understanding.

Living an Intuitive Life: A Path to Freedom

Living an intuitive life doesn't mean abandoning logic or reason. It means integrating intuition into your decision-making process, recognizing when the mind is useful and when it's getting in the way. By trusting intuition, you allow yourself to live with greater freedom, confidence, and authenticity.

When we live intuitively, we stop trying to control every outcome. We trust that even if we can't see the full picture, we are being guided by an inner wisdom that knows what is best for us. This creates a sense of flow in life—decisions become easier, opportunities appear more effortlessly, and we feel more aligned with our true selves.

An intuitive life is a life lived in harmony with who we really are. It's a life where we act from a place of trust, knowing that we are capable of navigating the unknown without constant mental interference. It's a life that embraces the mystery of the journey, where each step leads us closer to our highest potential.

Practical Steps to Strengthen Intuition

To cultivate and trust your intuition, try incorporating the following practices into your daily life:

- **Spend Time in Stillness**

Create moments of quiet throughout your day to listen to your inner voice. This could be through meditation, sitting in nature, or simply taking a few minutes to breathe deeply and center yourself.

- **Follow Your Hunches**

Start small by acting on your intuitive nudges in everyday situations. Whether it's choosing a book, deciding what to eat, or selecting a route to work, trust your instincts without overthinking.

- **Journal Your Insights**

Keep a journal where you record moments of intuitive insight. Over time, you'll start to see patterns and gain more confidence in your intuitive abilities.

- **Pay Attention to Your Body**

Notice how your body responds when faced with a decision. Does it feel tight and constricted, or light and open? These physical cues can help guide you toward the right choice.

- **Engage in Creative Play**

Explore creative activities that allow your mind to relax and your intuition to flow. Whether it's painting, writing, or simply daydreaming, give yourself permission to think outside the box.

Embracing Intuition as a Way of Life

Trusting intuition is about more than just making decisions—it's about living in alignment with your true self. By learning to quiet the mind and listen to your inner wisdom, you open yourself up to a life of greater clarity, freedom, and fulfillment.

As you continue to practice tuning into your intuition, remember that it's a journey. There will be times when doubt creeps in, and moments when you question whether you're on the right path. But with each decision you make from a place of intuition, you build trust in yourself and your ability to navigate life with grace and authenticity.

An intuitive life is a life lived in flow—where each step feels guided, where challenges become opportunities for growth, and where you move through the world with a sense of confidence and ease. Embrace your intuition, and let it lead you to a life that is aligned with your deepest truths.

CHAPTER 14

FOLLOWING THE FLOW: HOW TO LET YOUR INNER VOICE LEAD

The Dance of Inner Flow

Imagine a river flowing effortlessly through a valley. It twists and turns, sometimes encountering rocks, sometimes meandering through wide-open spaces. The river doesn't stop to overanalyze its course. It doesn't question whether it's taking the right path. It simply flows, trusting the natural pull of gravity and the terrain to guide it. This is what it means to follow the flow.

In our own lives, we often face the challenge of finding our flow—the natural rhythm of life that allows us to move forward with ease, without resistance or overthinking. When we follow the flow, we are led by our inner voice, a deep intuitive sense that knows where we need to go even when our minds are filled with doubt or confusion.

In this chapter, we explore what it means to follow the flow of life, learning to trust our inner voice as a guide. We'll dive into the practices that allow us to align with this flow, embracing life's natural currents without constantly swimming against them. By following the flow, we open ourselves to a life of greater ease, creativity, and purpose.

What Is the Flow? A State of Alignment

Flow, in its simplest form, is a state of alignment with the natural rhythm of life. It's that sense of being fully present, where everything seems to fall into place effortlessly. Athletes experience this when they are "in the zone," artists when they are deeply immersed in their craft, and writers when the words seem to write themselves. In these moments, time becomes fluid, and the distinction between ourselves and what we are doing dissolves. We are no longer forcing things to happen—we are simply allowing them to unfold.

But flow isn't just for athletes, artists, or creators. We all experience it, whether in moments of deep conversation, during a peaceful walk in nature, or while engaged in a task that feels purposeful and fulfilling. Flow is available to all of us, and it's something we can cultivate.

At its core, flow is about trusting in the process of life. It's about letting go of the need to control every detail and allowing our inner voice—the voice of intuition and deeper knowing—to guide our actions and decisions. When we're in flow, we're not overthinking or second-guessing ourselves. We're present, engaged, and aligned with what feels right, even if it doesn't always make sense to the rational mind.

The Inner Voice: Tuning into Your Personal Compass

We all have an inner voice, that quiet whisper that offers guidance from within. This voice is distinct from the mental chatter that often clouds our judgment. It's not the same as the loud, anxious voice of fear or doubt, nor is it the voice of external expectations or societal pressures. Instead, the inner voice is calm, steady, and persistent. It speaks with clarity, even when it's hard to hear amidst the noise of daily life.

Your inner voice is your personal compass, guiding you toward decisions and actions that are in alignment with your true self. But to hear it, you must learn to tune in. This requires practice, patience, and, most importantly, trust. When we're used to relying on external advice or overthinking every decision, it can be difficult to trust that quiet voice inside us.

The inner voice often communicates in subtle ways—a gut feeling, a sense of peace, a pull toward a certain direction. It doesn't always provide detailed explanations or logical reasons, but it's usually right. The more we practice listening to this voice, the stronger it becomes.

How Mental Resistance Blocks Flow

Flow is natural. It's how life wants to move through us when we're not resisting it. But often, our minds get in the way. We create resistance through overthinking, doubt, fear of failure, or the need to control every outcome. This mental resistance blocks the flow, making us feel stuck, frustrated, or disconnected from ourselves.

Think about a time when you felt out of sync—when nothing seemed to go right, and no matter how hard you tried, things didn't fall into place. This is what happens when we push against the natural flow. The mind takes over, creating rigid expectations about how things should be, rather than allowing life to unfold as it is.

One of the most common forms of mental resistance is the need for certainty. We want to know exactly how things will turn out before we act. We want guarantees of success or happiness before we commit to a decision. But life doesn't work that way. Flow requires trust—trust in ourselves, trust in the process, and trust that things will work out as they're meant to, even if we can't see the whole picture yet.

The Art of Letting Go: Releasing Control to Find Flow

Letting go is one of the hardest but most important practices for following the flow. It means releasing our tight grip on outcomes, letting go of the need to control every detail, and trusting that our inner voice knows the way. Letting go doesn't mean giving up—it means surrendering to the natural course of life, allowing ourselves to be guided rather than forcing things to happen.

When we let go, we stop swimming against the current. We stop trying to manipulate or control circumstances and instead learn to move with them. This doesn't mean we become passive or indifferent. On the contrary, letting go allows us to act from a place of clarity and purpose. We're no longer driven by fear or attachment; we're guided by our inner knowing.

Letting go requires a shift in mindset. Instead of focusing on what we want to achieve or avoid, we focus on how we can stay present and engaged in the moment. We learn to trust that the right opportunities, people, and experiences will come into our lives when we align with our flow, rather than when we try to force them.

Practical Steps to Follow the Flow

Learning to follow the flow is an ongoing practice, one that requires mindfulness, trust, and self-awareness. Here are some practical steps to help you connect with your inner voice and let your flow guide you:

- **Start with Stillness**

To hear your inner voice, you need to quiet the mind. Set aside time each day to practice stillness, whether through meditation, deep breathing, or simply sitting in nature. The more you cultivate inner stillness, the easier it becomes to recognize the flow when it arises.

- **Release Expectations**

One of the biggest blocks to flow is rigid expectations. When you find yourself attached to a specific outcome, try to release your grip on it. Remind yourself that life often unfolds in ways that are beyond your control, and that the journey is just as important as the destination.

- **Follow What Feels Right**

Instead of overthinking every decision, start tuning into how you feel. Pay attention to the subtle sensations in your body. Does a certain choice feel light, expansive, or energizing? Or does it feel heavy, constricting, or draining? Use these feelings as a guide to follow your flow.

- **Practice Patience**

Flow doesn't always happen on your timeline. Sometimes, life asks us to wait, to trust, and to allow things to unfold in their own time. Practice patience and remember that rushing or forcing things rarely leads to alignment.

- **Take Small Steps**

You don't need to make huge, life-altering decisions to follow the flow. Start small by listening to your intuition in everyday choices—whether it's choosing how to spend your free time, which projects to pursue, or how to handle a conversation. The more you practice following the flow in small moments, the more naturally it will come in larger decisions.

The Courage to Trust the Unknown

One of the greatest challenges of following the flow is the willingness to trust the unknown. Flow often leads us into uncharted territory, guiding us toward paths we hadn't considered or that feel uncertain. It asks us to step beyond our comfort zone, to trust that the inner voice knows more than the mind can comprehend.

This requires courage—the courage to act without knowing exactly how things will turn out, the courage to trust that we're being led in the right direction, even when we can't see the destination. Following the flow means being willing to let go of the need for guarantees and embracing the adventure of life as it unfolds.

When we trust the unknown, we open ourselves to new possibilities, experiences, and opportunities that we might never have encountered if we had stuck rigidly to our plans. The beauty of flow is that it often takes us to places we couldn't have predicted, but that are exactly where we need to be.

How to Know When You're in Flow

You'll know you're in flow when life starts to feel more effortless. This doesn't mean everything will be easy or that you won't face challenges, but it does mean that things will feel aligned. You'll notice synchronicities—unexpected opportunities, helpful people, or lucky breaks that seem to appear at just the right time. You'll feel more connected to yourself and to the world around you.

When you're in flow, decision-making becomes easier. You stop second-guessing yourself or overanalyzing every choice. Instead, you feel a deep sense of trust in your inner voice, knowing that it will guide you where you need to go. You act from a place of clarity and purpose, without the constant mental interference of doubt or fear.

Flow also brings a sense of joy and fulfillment. Even when you're working hard or facing obstacles, there's a feeling of rightness—a sense that you're exactly where you need to be, doing exactly what you need to do.

Living in Flow: A Lifelong Practice

Following the flow is not a one-time decision—it's a lifelong practice. It's about learning to trust your inner voice in every aspect of life, from the small everyday choices to the big life-changing decisions. It's about letting go of the need for control and learning to move with life's natural rhythms.

This practice requires patience, trust, and self-compassion. There will be times when you fall out of flow, when fear or doubt takes over, and that's okay. The key is to gently guide yourself back, to listen once again to the inner voice and follow its lead.

As you continue to practice following the flow, you'll find that life becomes more aligned, more joyful, and more meaningful. You'll experience a deeper connection to yourself, to others, and to the world around you. Most importantly, you'll discover that the flow is always there—ready to guide you whenever you're willing to listen.

Trusting the Flow of Life

The flow of life is always moving, always guiding us toward what is most aligned with our true selves. By learning to trust this flow and follow our inner voice, we open ourselves to a life of greater ease, clarity, and purpose. We stop fighting against the current and start moving with it, allowing life to unfold in ways that are often more beautiful and fulfilling than we could have imagined.

As you practice following the flow, remember that it's not about perfection. It's about presence—being fully engaged in the moment and trusting that your inner voice will lead you where you need to go. The more you listen, the stronger that voice becomes, and the more naturally you'll move through life with grace and confidence.

Let the flow guide you, and you'll discover a life that feels deeply aligned with who you truly are.

CHAPTER 15

MAKING ROOM FOR MIRACLES: CREATING SPACE FOR POSSIBILITIES

The Miracles We Overlook

L ife is filled with miracles. Some are grand and unmistakable, like the birth of a child, while others are quieter and subtler—a sunrise, a moment of unexpected kindness, or the feeling of peace that washes over us in a time of chaos. But most of us are too busy, too distracted, or too caught up in the day-to-day grind to notice these miracles. In the rush to meet deadlines, fulfill responsibilities, and chase our goals, we often miss the opportunities, the synchronicities, and the quiet miracles that life places in our path.

This chapter is about **making room for miracles**, about consciously creating space in your life for the unexpected, the awe-inspiring, and the transformative. It's about recognizing that when we slow down, simplify, and clear the clutter—both mental and physical—miracles naturally begin to occur. When we stop trying to control every detail of our lives and instead open ourselves to possibility, we invite in new experiences, opportunities, and connections that we might never have anticipated.

Creating space for miracles is not about magical thinking or waiting for life to hand us what we want on a silver platter. Rather, it's about cultivating a mindset of openness, trust, and readiness, so that when life's miracles do arrive, we are fully present and prepared to receive them.

The Nature of Miracles: Everyday Wonders

When we think of miracles, we often think of dramatic, life-changing events—someone recovering from a terminal illness, an unexpected windfall, or a near-impossible dream coming true. But miracles aren't always about defying the laws of nature or experiencing something extraordinary. In fact, the most powerful miracles are often the ones that go unnoticed—the ones that occur in the quiet, ordinary moments of life.

Consider the miracle of breathing. Every breath you take is a complex, finely tuned process that sustains your life. Or the miracle of connection—the way we can reach out and touch the heart of another person through a simple gesture of kindness or understanding. These everyday miracles may seem small, but they are profound reminders of the beauty and wonder that surrounds us at all times.

To make room for miracles, we must first redefine what we consider miraculous. We must learn to recognize the magic in the mundane, to appreciate the countless ways life supports and sustains us, even in the most challenging times. This shift in perspective allows us to see that miracles are not rare occurrences, but a natural part of life when we are open to them.

The Clutter That Blocks Miracles

One of the greatest barriers to experiencing miracles is clutter—both physical and mental. When our lives are filled with too much stuff, too many distractions, or too many obligations, we leave little room for the unexpected to enter. Clutter creates noise, and in that noise, it becomes difficult to hear the whispers of possibility or notice the subtle nudges of intuition that guide us toward new opportunities.

Physical Clutter

Physical clutter is easy to recognize. It's the piles of papers on your desk, the overflowing closet, or the never-ending to-do list. It's the stuff that fills your space and weighs on your mind, making it hard to think clearly or find peace. When our physical environment is cluttered, it reflects a state of internal disorganization. We feel scattered, overwhelmed, and closed off from the flow of life.

To create space for miracles, it's essential to clear out the physical clutter. This doesn't mean you have to become a minimalist, but it does mean being intentional about what you keep and what you let go of. When you clear your space, you make room for new energy, new ideas, and new possibilities to enter your life.

Mental Clutter

Mental clutter is more subtle but equally, if not more, impactful. It's the constant stream of thoughts, worries, and distractions that fill your mind. It's the overthinking, the fear of failure, and the limiting beliefs that keep you stuck in the same patterns. Mental clutter keeps you focused on the past or future, preventing you from being fully present in the moment.

When your mind is cluttered, it's hard to recognize the miracles that are already happening in your life. You might miss the small synchronicities or the opportunities that arise because you're too busy worrying about what might go wrong or replaying past mistakes. Clearing mental clutter involves quieting the mind, letting go of unhelpful thoughts, and practicing mindfulness to stay present.

Clearing Space for Miracles: Practical Steps

Creating space for miracles requires both inner and outer work. It's about making physical and mental room for new possibilities, but it's also about cultivating an attitude of openness and trust. Here are some practical steps you can take to begin making room for miracles in your life:

Simplify Your Space

Start by decluttering your physical environment. Go through your home or workspace and let go of anything that no longer serves you. This doesn't have to be a massive overhaul, but even small changes can make a big difference. When your space is clear and organized, you'll feel lighter, more focused, and more open to new experiences.

Quiet the Mind

Mental clutter often arises from the need to control or predict the future. To make room for miracles, practice letting go of the need for certainty. Engage in mindfulness or meditation practices to help quiet the mind and bring your focus back to the present moment. The more present you are, the more attuned you'll be to the possibilities that surround you.

Let Go of Attachment

Attachment to specific outcomes can block the flow of miracles. When you're too focused on how things *should* be, you close yourself off to how they *could* be. Practice releasing your attachment to particular results and instead trust that the universe has something even better in store for you. This openness creates the space for unexpected blessings to enter your life.

Cultivate Gratitude

Gratitude is one of the most powerful ways to invite more miracles into your life. When you focus on what you already have, rather than what's lacking, you shift your energy to a place of abundance. Gratitude opens your heart and mind, making it easier to recognize the miracles that are already present and attracting even more into your experience.

The Power of Openness: Inviting the Unseen

When we create space in our lives, we invite in possibilities that we may not have considered. Openness is a state of being that allows for growth, expansion, and transformation. It's about being willing to say yes to life, even when we don't know exactly where it will lead us.

Openness requires trust—trust in ourselves, trust in the process, and trust that the universe is working in our favor. When we approach life with an open heart and mind, we are more likely to see opportunities that others may overlook. We are more willing to take risks, try new things, and step into the unknown, knowing that something miraculous might be waiting for us on the other side.

But openness also requires us to let go of our need for control. It's about surrendering to the flow of life and allowing things to unfold naturally. When we stop trying to force outcomes or micromanage every detail, we make room for the unexpected—miracles that we couldn't have planned for but that enrich our lives in profound ways.

Trusting the Process: The Key to Allowing Miracles

Trust is a central theme in making room for miracles. Without trust, it's easy to fall into doubt, fear, or impatience. We become fixated on the idea that things aren't happening fast enough or that we need to take control to make things happen. But miracles often require time and space to unfold. They happen when we allow, not when we force.

To cultivate trust, start by recognizing that life has its own rhythm and timing. Sometimes, things don't happen when or how we expect, but that doesn't mean they aren't happening. Miracles often come in unexpected ways and at unexpected times, and our job is to stay open and ready to receive them.

One way to build trust is to reflect on past experiences when something miraculous or unexpected occurred. Perhaps it was a time when you met the right person at exactly the right moment or when a solution appeared out of nowhere just when you needed it. These moments remind us that life is full of unseen forces working behind the scenes, guiding us toward what we need.

Zen and Miracles: Embracing the Unknown

Zen philosophy teaches us to embrace the unknown, to live fully in the present moment without attachment to outcomes. In Zen, there is a focus on the practice of **non-doing**—the idea that sometimes the most powerful action is to do nothing, to simply allow life to unfold as it will. This doesn't mean being passive, but rather being fully engaged in the moment without trying to control it.

This Zen approach to life is closely aligned with making room for miracles. When we stop striving, pushing, and forcing, we create space for the miraculous to happen. When we let go of our need to know how everything will turn out, we open ourselves to new possibilities, new insights, and new paths.

As we practice being present and embracing the unknown, we begin to see that life is constantly offering us gifts—gifts of wisdom, growth, and opportunity. These are the miracles that arise when we make space for them, when we are open to receiving whatever life has in store for us.

Miracles in Relationships: Making Space for Connection

Miracles don't just happen in our personal lives; they also happen in our relationships. When we create space for connection, we invite in the possibility of deep, meaningful relationships with others. But too often, our relationships are cluttered with expectations, judgments, or past hurts that prevent us from truly connecting.

To make room for miracles in relationships, it's important to let go of old stories and patterns that no longer serve us. This might mean forgiving someone who hurt us, releasing resentment, or letting go of unrealistic expectations. When we clear this emotional clutter, we create space for new energy to enter our relationships—energy that allows for healing, growth, and transformation.

Being open and vulnerable in relationships also invites miracles. When we are willing to be seen as we truly are, without hiding behind masks or walls, we create the possibility for deep connection. This openness allows us to experience the miracle of being fully known and fully loved, just as we are.

Living a Life of Possibility: The Miracle of Potential

When we make room for miracles, we are essentially making room for possibility. We are opening ourselves to the potential that life offers us in every moment. This doesn't mean that every day will be filled with dramatic or life-changing events, but it does mean that we live with a sense of wonder, curiosity, and openness to whatever may come.

Living a life of possibility means approaching each day with a beginner's mind—seeing the world as if for the first time, free from the limitations of past experiences or future expectations. It's about being willing to take risks, to try new things, and to embrace the unknown, knowing that even the smallest action can lead to something extraordinary.

The miracle of potential is always present. It's in the choices we make, the actions we take, and the thoughts we think. Every moment holds the potential for something new, something miraculous, to unfold. And when we create space for that potential, we invite more of it into our lives.

Practical Steps to Invite Miracles Into Your Life

Here are some practical steps you can take to create space for miracles and possibilities:

Declutter Your Life

Clear out the physical, emotional, and mental clutter that is taking up space in your life. This might mean cleaning your home, letting go of old grudges, or simplifying your schedule. When you clear out the old, you make room for the new.

Practice Mindfulness

Mindfulness helps you stay present and open to the miracles happening around you. Set aside time each day to practice being fully present, whether through meditation, mindful breathing, or simply noticing the beauty in your surroundings.

Trust the Timing of Your Life

Let go of the need to control or force outcomes. Trust that life is unfolding in its own perfect timing, even if it doesn't always align with your expectations. The more you trust, the more open you become to the unexpected gifts that life offers.

Stay Curious

Cultivate a sense of curiosity and wonder about life. Approach each day with an open heart and mind, ready to explore new possibilities. Curiosity invites miracles because it keeps you open to what's possible, rather than fixated on what's known.

A Life Full of Miracles

Making room for miracles is about creating space—space in your mind, in your heart, and in your life for the unexpected to enter. It's about recognizing that life is full of possibilities, and that when we clear the clutter and let go of control, we invite in experiences and opportunities that we could never have imagined.

As you practice making room for miracles, remember that they don't always arrive in dramatic or obvious ways. Sometimes, the most profound miracles are the quietest—the ones that unfold slowly, gently, and with grace. But the more space you create, the more you'll begin to notice them, and the more your life will be filled with a sense of wonder, joy, and possibility

CHAPTER 16

THE JOURNEY OF NON-THINKING OVERCOMING OBSTACLES

The Paradox of Non-Thinking

In a world where thinking is prized, the idea of "non-thinking" may seem counterintuitive. We are taught to solve problems with our intellect, analyze situations from every angle, and come up with carefully reasoned decisions. Yet, there is an ancient wisdom that suggests something different: the idea that true clarity and peace come not from thinking harder, but from thinking less—or even, at times, not thinking at all.

This chapter is about the **journey of non-thinking**, a practice that allows us to overcome the mental obstacles that block our path to peace, creativity, and insight. Non-thinking is not about abandoning thought entirely, but about recognizing when our minds are overactive and letting go of the mental chatter that often leads to stress, confusion, or frustration. By learning to quiet the mind and step away from the compulsion to overthink, we create space for deeper awareness, intuition, and flow.

We'll explore how the practice of non-thinking can help you overcome the obstacles that arise on your path—whether they be internal (such as fear, doubt, or limiting beliefs) or external (such as unexpected setbacks or difficult situations). By examining both the benefits and challenges of non-thinking, this chapter will guide you toward a more balanced and peaceful approach to life.

What Is Non-Thinking? A State Beyond the Mind

Non-thinking doesn't mean turning off your brain or ignoring reality. Instead, it's about shifting from a mode of constant mental processing to a state of presence and awareness. In this state, you're not consumed by the need to label, judge, or analyze every situation. Instead, you allow things to be as they are, observing without attaching to thoughts.

Non-thinking is often compared to a state of flow, where actions come naturally and effortlessly, unimpeded by overthinking or mental noise. In this state, the mind becomes clear and calm, like a still lake that reflects everything around it without distortion. While it may sound like an abstract concept, non-thinking is something we've all experienced—perhaps during moments of deep relaxation, while immersed in nature, or during creative activities when time seems to disappear.

Zen teachings emphasize this state of non-thinking, often referring to it as **no-mind** or **mushin**. Zen Master Takuan Sōhō described this state as

"mind without mind,"

where there is no separation between the individual and their actions, and everything happens with natural ease. It is not the absence of thought but the absence of attachment to thought.

The Obstacles of Thinking: When the Mind Becomes a Barrier

The mind is a powerful tool, capable of reasoning, imagining, and solving complex problems. However, it can also become a source of suffering when overused or misused. Many of the obstacles we face in life are not external, but internal—rooted in the way we think about situations, events, and ourselves.

Overthinking and Analysis Paralysis

One of the most common obstacles to non-thinking is **overthinking**. This occurs when the mind becomes trapped in a cycle of endless analysis, rehashing the same thoughts and worries over and over. Overthinking often leads to **analysis paralysis**, where you become so consumed with evaluating every possible option or outcome that you fail to make any decision at all.

While careful thought can be beneficial, overthinking often creates more confusion than clarity. The more you think, the more complex the situation seems, and the more distant the solution feels. Overthinking can make even simple decisions feel overwhelming, and it often leads to stress, anxiety, and frustration.

Advantages of Overthinking:

- Helps in complex situations requiring detailed analysis.

- Encourages thorough exploration of all possible outcomes.

Disadvantages of Overthinking:

- Can create unnecessary stress and anxiety.

- May lead to indecision or missed opportunities.

- Often distracts from the simplicity of the present moment.

Mental Noise and Distraction

In today's fast-paced world, we are constantly bombarded with information, distractions, and noise—both externally from technology and media, and internally from our own thoughts. This **mental noise** can prevent us from accessing deeper insights or connecting with our intuition. When the mind is cluttered with thoughts, it becomes difficult to focus, make clear decisions, or find peace.

Mental noise can take many forms—worrying about the future, replaying past events, comparing yourself to others, or ruminating on "what if" scenarios. All of these thoughts clutter the mind and create obstacles to clarity and calm.

Advantages of Mental Noise:

- Keeps the brain stimulated and engaged.

- Encourages creative problem-solving in fast-paced environments.

Disadvantages of Mental Noise:

- Can lead to burnout and overwhelm.

- Blocks access to intuition and deeper awareness.

- Makes it harder to focus on the present and enjoy life.

Overcoming Obstacles Through Non-Thinking

Non-thinking offers a way to overcome these mental obstacles by helping us step out of the cycle of over-analysis, noise, and distraction. Through the practice of non-thinking, we can cultivate greater clarity, peace, and resilience in the face of life's challenges.

Quieting the Mind Through Mindfulness

Mindfulness is one of the most effective tools for practicing non-thinking. By focusing your attention on the present moment—whether it's your breath, the sounds around you, or the sensations in your body—you can begin to quiet the constant chatter of the mind.

Mindfulness teaches you to observe thoughts without getting caught up in them. Instead of following every thought to its conclusion, you learn to let thoughts come and go, like clouds passing through the sky. This detachment from thought creates space for greater clarity and insight to arise.

Advantages of Mindfulness:

- Reduces stress and anxiety by calming the mind.

- Enhances focus and concentration.

- Encourages a deeper connection to the present moment.

Challenges of Mindfulness:

- Requires consistent practice and patience.

- May be difficult in moments of high stress or emotional turmoil.

Embracing Uncertainty

One of the reasons we cling to overthinking is that we fear uncertainty. We believe that if we think enough, we can control or predict the outcome of a situation. But in reality, life is full of uncertainty, and no amount of thinking can eliminate that.

The journey of non-thinking involves embracing uncertainty and letting go of the need for control. Instead of trying to predict or manipulate outcomes, you allow life to unfold naturally, trusting that you will be able to handle whatever comes your way.

This doesn't mean ignoring problems or acting recklessly. Instead, it's about recognizing that not every situation requires a solution or explanation right away. By accepting uncertainty, you free yourself from the mental burden of trying to control the uncontrollable.

Advantages of Embracing Uncertainty:

- Reduces the pressure to have all the answers.

- Opens the door to new possibilities and creative solutions.

Challenges of Embracing Uncertainty:

- Can feel uncomfortable, especially for those who prefer control or structure.

- May require a shift in mindset and letting go of deeply ingrained beliefs.

Cultivating Presence in Action

Zen practice often emphasizes the idea of **being fully present** in whatever you're doing, whether it's washing the dishes, walking, or having a conversation. This state of presence is closely linked to non-thinking because when you are fully engaged in the present moment, the mind has less room to wander or overthink.

When you are fully present, there is no need to analyze, compare, or judge. You simply do what needs to be done, trusting that your actions will flow naturally and effortlessly. This presence in action leads to a state of **effortless doing**, where everything feels aligned and in harmony.

Advantages of Presence in Action:

- Increases productivity and enjoyment of tasks.

- Reduces mental clutter and distractions.

Challenges of Presence in Action:

- Difficult to maintain when multitasking or under stress.

- Requires practice to develop and sustain.

Zen Teachings on Non-Thinking: Lessons from the Masters

The practice of non-thinking is deeply rooted in Zen philosophy, which teaches us to step beyond the mind and into a state of pure awareness. Zen Masters throughout history have offered guidance on how to navigate the obstacles of overthinking and mental noise, providing timeless wisdom for those seeking clarity and peace.

Zen Master **Dogen**, one of the most influential figures in Zen Buddhism, famously said,

"To study the way is to study the self. To study the self
is to forget the self."

This teaching reminds us that non-thinking is not about ignoring the mind, but about seeing beyond the ego-driven thoughts that cloud our awareness. When we forget the self—our fears, doubts, and attachments—we create space for deeper wisdom to emerge.

Another Zen teaching emphasizes the importance of **non-attachment to thought**. As Zen Master **Shunryu Suzuki** said, "In the beginner's mind there are many possibilities, but in the expert's mind there are few." The beginner's mind is one that is free from rigid beliefs and preconceived notions, open to new experiences and insights. By approaching life with a beginner's mind, we are less likely to get stuck in overthinking and more likely to see things with fresh eyes.

Non-Thinking as a Path to Freedom

Ultimately, the journey of non-thinking is a path to freedom—freedom from the mental obstacles that keep us stuck in fear, doubt, or indecision. It is a practice of letting go, not just of thoughts, but of the need to control, judge, or fix everything.

When we learn to step beyond the, **judge, or fix everything**, we open ourselves to a deeper sense of peace and flow in life. This freedom isn't about ignoring reality or refusing to engage with life's challenges. Rather, it's about meeting those challenges from a place of inner stillness and clarity, unclouded by the mental noise that often overwhelms us.

Non-thinking allows us to move through life with a sense of lightness. We no longer carry the heavy burden of constant over-analysis or the endless mental loops that tell us we haven't done enough or that we aren't enough. Instead, we find the courage to let go, to trust in ourselves and in life's unfolding, and to act from a place of deep, intuitive wisdom.

How Non-Thinking Helps Overcome Internal Obstacles

Life presents many challenges, both external and internal. The external obstacles are often easier to identify—difficult circumstances, unexpected setbacks, or conflicts with others. However, the internal obstacles, such as fear, self-doubt, and limiting beliefs, can be far more insidious and difficult to overcome. Non-thinking offers a way to address these internal barriers by bypassing the mental patterns that reinforce them.

Overcoming Fear Through Stillness

Fear is one of the most common internal obstacles we face. Whether it's fear of failure, fear of judgment, or fear of the unknown, it often manifests as overthinking. We try to think our way out of fear, attempting to plan for every possible outcome or control every variable. But this mental approach only deepens our anxiety, as we quickly realize that no amount of thinking can guarantee safety or certainty.

Non-thinking offers a different approach to fear. Instead of trying to rationalize our way out of it, we simply observe the fear without judgment or attachment. We allow the fear to be present, but we don't let it dictate our actions or paralyze us. In this way, we create space for courage to arise naturally, without the interference of overactive thoughts.

When we stop feeding fear with endless mental chatter, we often find that it loses its power. The clarity that comes from non-thinking helps us see that many of our fears are rooted in false assumptions or exaggerated worst-case scenarios. By quieting the mind, we allow ourselves to respond to fear with calmness and clarity, rather than reactivity and panic.

2. Dissolving Self-Doubt Through Acceptance

Self-doubt is another powerful internal obstacle that can keep us stuck in cycles of overthinking and hesitation. When we doubt ourselves, we often become trapped in mental loops, questioning every decision and second-guessing our abilities. This self-doubt can be paralyzing, preventing us from taking action or pursuing our goals.

The practice of non-thinking helps dissolve self-doubt by fostering acceptance. Instead of fighting against our doubts or trying to reason them away, we learn to accept them as part of the human experience. We acknowledge the presence of doubt, but we don't let it define us or control our actions.

By letting go of the need to overthink every decision, we begin to trust ourselves more fully. We come to realize that self-doubt is often just a product of the mind, not an accurate reflection of our true capabilities. In the space created by non-thinking, we can reconnect with our inner confidence and move forward with a sense of trust in ourselves.

Releasing Limiting Beliefs Through Awareness

Limiting beliefs are deeply ingrained thought patterns that hold us back from reaching our full potential. These beliefs often operate below the surface of our conscious awareness, shaping our decisions and actions in subtle but powerful ways. Examples of limiting beliefs include thoughts like "I'm not good enough," "I don't deserve success," or "It's too late for me to change."

Non-thinking helps us release limiting beliefs by bringing them into the light of awareness. When we stop identifying so strongly with our thoughts, we can begin to see these beliefs for what they are—mental constructs that are not necessarily true. Through mindfulness and non-attachment to thought, we create the mental space to question and challenge these limiting beliefs.

As we practice non-thinking, we start to notice the patterns of thought that have been running our lives. We see how certain beliefs have kept us small, fearful, or stuck. In the clarity of non-thinking, we can choose to let go of these beliefs and replace them with more empowering ones.

Zen Approach to Overcoming External Obstacles

While non-thinking is invaluable for addressing internal obstacles, it also provides a powerful framework for navigating external challenges. Life is unpredictable, and we all encounter obstacles—whether in the form of difficult circumstances, conflict with others, or unexpected setbacks. The Zen approach to non-thinking offers a way to face these challenges with grace and resilience.

Responding, Not Reacting

One of the key teachings in Zen is the difference between reacting and responding. When we react to external obstacles, we often do so impulsively, driven by emotion or mental habits. Reactions are immediate, unthinking, and often unhelpful. They are driven by the ego, which seeks to protect itself from discomfort or threat.

Non-thinking allows us to cultivate the ability to **respond** rather than react. In a state of non-thinking, we pause before taking action, allowing ourselves to fully experience the moment without being swept away by emotions or mental patterns. This pause creates space for a more thoughtful and effective response, one that comes from a place of clarity rather than reactivity.

Zen Master **Thich Nhat Hanh** often spoke of the importance of mindfulness in responding to life's challenges. He taught that by staying present and aware, we can respond to difficulties with compassion, wisdom, and calmness. This mindful approach to external obstacles helps us navigate even the most challenging situations with grace.

Letting Go of Resistance

Another key aspect of the Zen approach to overcoming obstacles is the practice of **letting go of resistance**. When we encounter external obstacles, our first instinct is often to resist them—to push back, to fight against the situation, or to try to force things to go our way. This resistance creates tension, frustration, and often makes the obstacle feel even more insurmountable.

Non-thinking teaches us to let go of this resistance and instead accept the situation as it is. This doesn't mean giving up or being passive. Rather, it means recognizing that resistance only creates more suffering. By accepting the reality of the obstacle, we can find a way to move forward without being weighed down by frustration or anger.

As Zen Master **Shunryu Suzuki** said,

> *"Life is like stepping onto a boat which is about to sail out to sea and sink."*

This quote reminds us that life is unpredictable and full of challenges, and that the key to peace lies in accepting this reality rather than fighting against it. When we let go of the need for life to be a certain way, we free ourselves from the suffering that comes with resistance.

The Practice of Non-Thinking: Practical Applications

While the concept of non-thinking may seem abstract, it can be applied in very practical ways to everyday life. Whether you're facing a difficult decision, dealing with a challenging relationship, or simply trying to find more peace in your day-to-day life, the practice of non-thinking can help you navigate these situations with greater clarity and ease.

Non-Thinking in Decision-Making

When faced with a difficult decision, it's easy to fall into the trap of overthinking—trying to predict every possible outcome, weighing the pros and cons endlessly, and feeling overwhelmed by the pressure to make the "right" choice. Non-thinking offers a different approach.

Instead of trying to think your way to a solution, try stepping back from the problem and allowing your mind to rest. Engage in a simple activity, such as taking a walk or focusing on your breath, and allow the decision to simmer in the background. Often, the clarity you're seeking will arise naturally when you stop trying to force it.

Non-Thinking in Relationships

Relationships can be a major source of mental and emotional stress, especially when we get caught up in overthinking conflicts, misunderstandings, or expectations. Non-thinking can help you approach relationships with more presence and openness.

When conflicts arise, practice stepping away from the mental storylines and judgments that fuel the conflict. Instead, focus on listening deeply to the other person and observing your own emotions without reacting to them. This creates space for more authentic communication and connection.

Non-Thinking in Daily Life

The practice of non-thinking can be integrated into the simplest aspects of daily life, whether you're cooking, cleaning, working, or driving. By bringing mindful awareness to whatever you're doing, you can quiet the mental noise and enter a state of flow. In this state, tasks that once felt mundane or stressful become opportunities for presence and peace.

The Ongoing Journey of Non-Thinking

The journey of non-thinking is not a destination, but an ongoing practice. It's about learning to live with greater awareness, presence, and ease, free from the mental obstacles that often cloud our clarity and peace. While the path of non-thinking may be challenging at times—especially in a world that values constant thinking and doing—it offers profound rewards.

As you continue to practice non-thinking, you'll find that many of the obstacles you once faced—whether internal or external—begin to dissolve. You'll experience a greater sense of freedom, both from the mental patterns that once held you back and from the need to control or resist life's unfolding.

111

Zen Master **Dogen** said,

*"Do not follow the ideas of others, but learn to listen to
the voice within yourself."*

This is the essence of non-thinking—learning to quiet the mind and listen to the deeper wisdom that lies beyond thought. As you embark on this journey, remember that each moment is an opportunity to practice, and that with each step, you are moving closer to a life of greater clarity, peace, and freedom.

CHAPTER 17

THE JOURNEY OF NON-THINKING OVERCOMING OBSTACLES

Reaching the Edge of the Familiar

There comes a time in every journey when the path forward becomes less defined, where the familiar gives way to the unknown. You've spent time growing, evolving, and moving toward your goals, but as you approach the edge of what you know, a question arises: *What happens next?*

The horizon is not a final destination but a threshold—a gateway to the next phase of life. Stepping across this threshold brings a mix of excitement, anticipation, and uncertainty. It's a space filled with possibility, where new paths are waiting to be explored. But this moment also presents a challenge: how do you embrace the unknown, stay grounded in what you've learned, and remain open to what lies ahead?

In this chapter, we explore the concept of **new horizons**, the shifting landscapes of life, and how to navigate them with courage, curiosity, and an openness to what comes next. We'll examine how to face the uncertainty of this transition, how to expand your vision beyond the familiar, and how to continue growing even when the path forward isn't entirely clear.

A Horizon Is Not an Endpoint: It's a Beginning

Many people think of the horizon as a point to reach, a distant place where they'll finally find completion or fulfillment. But in reality, the horizon is always moving. As you approach it, it expands, revealing new challenges and opportunities, making it clear that the journey is never truly finished. In this sense, the horizon is not an endpoint but a constant beginning, a place from which new possibilities emerge.

Personal growth operates in the same way. Just when you think you've arrived—at a goal, a realization, or a new level of awareness—you discover that there's more to explore. This isn't a sign of failure or incompleteness; it's the natural rhythm of life. Each achievement, each milestone, opens the door to further growth. The horizon, much like life itself, is a space of continuous evolution, where each step forward leads to new discoveries.

Stepping Into the Unknown: A Necessary Leap

When you reach a new horizon, you are standing on the edge of the known world, looking out over territory that you've never crossed before. The ground beneath your feet feels solid, but the space ahead is vast and undefined. Stepping into this unknown requires **courage**—the kind of courage that comes from trusting in yourself and in the process of life.

The unknown is where possibilities flourish. It's where growth happens in ways that you could never plan or predict. Yet, many people fear the uncertainty that comes with crossing into this new space. We're often wired to cling to what's familiar, even if it no longer serves us, because the unknown feels risky and unsettling.

But the unknown is also where life's greatest adventures unfold. When you step into the unknown with a sense of curiosity, rather than fear, you give yourself the freedom to experience life in its fullness. This is where **transformation** happens—not through careful planning or staying within the boundaries of the familiar, but through embracing the unpredictable nature of what comes next.

Trusting Yourself and the Process

When you approach a new horizon, there's a natural temptation to try and plan everything out, to control the outcome, and to make sense of what lies ahead. But the truth is, some things cannot be planned or controlled. The future, in its uncertainty, holds surprises that are often beyond our ability to foresee. The key to navigating this uncertainty is trust—not only in the unfolding of life but also in your own ability to handle whatever comes next.

Trust is a powerful ally when facing the unknown. It's about believing that you have the inner resources to navigate whatever arises, even if the path is unclear. This trust is not built on certainty or guarantees; it's built on the understanding that you've faced uncertainty before and come through stronger, wiser, and more resilient.

This doesn't mean passivity or inaction. Trusting the process means being actively engaged with life but without the need to force or manipulate outcomes. It's about letting go of the need for control and allowing things to unfold naturally, trusting that the right path will reveal itself as you move forward.

The Space Between: Navigating the In-Between

One of the most challenging parts of reaching a new horizon is the transition phase—the **in-between** space where the old has fallen away, but the new has not yet fully emerged. This can be a time of uncertainty, where the future feels hazy and undefined. It's a space that can feel uncomfortable because it requires patience and openness without the clarity of what's next.

But the in-between is also a **fertile ground** for new possibilities. It's a time when you can reflect on the journey so far, integrate the lessons you've learned, and prepare yourself for what's to come. The key to navigating this space is presence—staying grounded in the moment, even when the future feels uncertain.

Rather than rushing to fill the space with answers or decisions, allow yourself to simply be in this moment of transition. Trust that clarity will come, but also recognize that this period of uncertainty is an essential part of the process. The in-between is where transformation happens—where you shed old identities, beliefs, or patterns, and make room for new growth.

Embracing New Possibilities: Expanding Your Vision

As you approach a new horizon, you're not only stepping into the unknown; you're also expanding your vision of what's possible. The possibilities that exist beyond the familiar are often greater than anything you could have imagined while standing in the past. When you allow yourself to embrace these possibilities, you open yourself to **new opportunities**, new relationships, and new ways of being.

But expanding your vision requires a willingness to step outside of your comfort zone. It means being open to the unexpected and willing to take risks. The path ahead may not look like what you envisioned, but that's often where the magic happens. Life has a way of surprising you when you're open to possibilities beyond what you currently know.

As you expand your vision, it's important to stay connected to your core values and desires. While the path may twist and turn in unexpected ways, having a clear sense of what matters most to you will help guide your decisions. What is it that truly inspires you? What are you passionate about? These questions will help you navigate new horizons with intention and purpose.

The Creative Potential of Uncertainty

While uncertainty can feel unsettling, it is also the source of **creative potential**. When we step into the unknown, we are no longer confined by the limits of what we think we know. This space allows for creativity to flourish in ways that it can't when we're trying to control every aspect of life. In uncertainty, there's room for new ideas, new perspectives, and new solutions to emerge.

Creativity thrives in the space between what was and what will be. As you move toward new horizons, tap into this creative energy. Allow yourself to imagine possibilities that are beyond your current reality. Ask yourself, *What could be?* instead of focusing on *What should be?*

This shift in perspective can lead to breakthroughs in areas where you may have felt stuck or limited. By embracing uncertainty as a space of creative potential, you give yourself the freedom to experiment, explore, and dream bigger than before.

Reflection as a Tool for Growth

As you approach new horizons, it's important to take time to reflect on the journey that has brought you to this point. Reflection is not about dwelling on the past, but about integrating the lessons you've learned and recognizing how far you've come. This reflection helps you move forward with a deeper understanding of yourself and your journey.

Consider the challenges you've faced, the obstacles you've overcome, and the growth you've experienced. What have these experiences taught you? How have they shaped who you are today? Reflection helps you carry forward the wisdom you've gained, ensuring that it informs your future choices and actions.

However, reflection is not the same as attachment. While it's important to honor your past, it's equally important to let go of any attachment to it. Clinging to old identities, achievements, or ways of being can prevent you from fully embracing the new possibilities that lie ahead. Reflection should serve as a

116

guide, not a tether.

Setting New Intentions: Planting Seeds for the Future

As you step into a new horizon, it's helpful to set **intentions** for what you want to create or experience in this next phase of life. Unlike rigid goals, which are often tied to specific outcomes, intentions are more about the **energy and focus** you bring to your journey. They serve as guiding principles that help you stay aligned with your values and purpose as you navigate the unknown.

Intentions are about direction, not destination. They help you remain grounded in what's important to you while leaving room for flexibility and spontaneity. What do you want to invite into your life? How do you want to feel as you move forward? What kind of growth are you seeking in this new chapter?

Setting intentions helps create a sense of purpose and clarity, even when the path ahead isn't entirely clear. It's a way of aligning your actions with your deepest desires, ensuring that you're moving toward what truly matters to you.

Moving Forward: Walking Into the Infinite Horizon

The journey toward new horizons is one of continuous discovery. Each horizon you reach opens up new possibilities, and with each step forward, the landscape changes. This is the beauty of life—it's a never-ending process of growth, exploration, and transformation.

What happens next? The answer is that no one can know for sure. But that's exactly what makes life so rich and exciting. The future is not something to be predicted or controlled; it's something to be lived. The new horizon invites you to step forward with curiosity, courage, and an open heart.

As you move forward, remember that the journey is the destination. Each moment, each decision, each experience contributes to the unfolding of your life. The horizon will always shift, but that's where the adventure lies. It's not about reaching a final goal, but about embracing the endless possibilities that each new horizon presents.

Embrace the Unknown With Open Arms

Reaching a new horizon is not the end of the journey, but the beginning of a new chapter. It's a moment to pause, reflect, and step into the unknown with a sense of trust and openness. The question, *What happens next?*, is not something to be feared but something to be embraced.

As you continue on your journey, remember that each new horizon brings with it the potential for growth, discovery, and transformation. Life is not about arriving at a final destination, but about continuously expanding, evolving, and becoming. The more you embrace the unknown, the more you'll find that the possibilities are truly limitless.

Step into the horizon with confidence. Trust the process. And allow yourself to be surprised by what happens next.

BEYOND THE MIND—ENDING SUFFERING THROUGH INNER PEACE

As we close this exploration of non-thinking and its power to transform the way we live, it is essential to revisit the fundamental message at the heart of this journey: **inner peace** cannot be found through external achievements, wealth, or even the resolution of all life's difficulties. True peace emerges when we learn to go **beyond the mind**, letting go of the ceaseless mental chatter, judgments, and anxieties that dominate our thoughts. By stepping beyond these confines, we free ourselves from the cycle of suffering and discover an enduring state of inner tranquility.

The Mind as a Source of Suffering

For many of us, the primary source of our suffering is not the events of the world but our **attachment to the narratives and judgments** created by our minds. The mind constantly weaves stories around every experience we encounter, defining situations as either good or bad, right or wrong, pleasurable or painful. In doing so, it creates endless cycles of joy followed by disappointment, satisfaction followed by anxiety. This endless loop of mental labeling keeps us trapped in a state of psychological tension, constantly oscillating between elation and despair.

But the truth is, these mental narratives are not reality. They are simply **interpretations**—mental filters through which we experience the world. The mind's tendency to assign meaning to every event leads to suffering because we become attached to these interpretations, often mistaking them for absolute truths. The practice of non-thinking, which we have examined throughout this book, offers a way to free ourselves from this cycle by **detaching from the mental constructs** that dominate our perception of reality.

Zen Master **Huang Po** once said,

> *"The foolish reject what they see, not what they think;*
> *the wise reject what they think, not what they see."*

119

This quote highlights the core issue: our suffering is rooted not in the reality of the world but in the thoughts and beliefs we form about that reality. By moving beyond the mind and releasing our attachment to these mental constructs, we can begin to experience the world as it is—free from the distortions created by our thinking.

The Illusion of Control: Letting Go of Mental Effort

A major source of suffering is our desire for **control**. The mind, in its attempt to protect us from harm, constantly seeks to plan, predict, and manipulate the future. It convinces us that by thinking through every scenario, we can avoid disappointment, prevent failure, and ensure success. But the truth is that life is inherently unpredictable, and no amount of mental effort can guarantee specific outcomes.

This illusion of control is a significant barrier to inner peace because it keeps us locked in a state of **constant mental effort**. We expend enormous energy trying to think our way to a future that aligns with our desires, only to find that life rarely unfolds exactly as planned. When things don't go our way, the mind responds with frustration, fear, or self-blame, deepening our suffering.

Non-thinking offers a powerful antidote to this cycle. By letting go of the need for control, we free ourselves from the mental strain of constantly trying to shape the future. Instead, we learn to **trust the flow of life**, understanding that while we cannot control every outcome, we can control how we respond to each moment. This shift in perspective allows us to experience greater ease and acceptance, even in the face of uncertainty.

Non-Thinking: The Path to Inner Freedom

The practice of non-thinking is not about emptying the mind of all thoughts; rather, it is about cultivating a sense of **inner freedom** by detaching from the constant stream of thoughts that arise. In this state, thoughts may come and go, but they no longer hold power over us. We are no longer dragged into mental narratives that fuel anxiety, frustration, or self-doubt. Instead, we remain grounded in the present moment, free from the need to engage with every passing thought.

This sense of inner freedom is one of the greatest gifts of non-thinking. It allows us to experience life with **clarity and presence**, unburdened by the weight of mental stories. In this state, we are better able to navigate challenges, make decisions, and respond to the world with wisdom and compassion.

The renowned spiritual teacher **Eckhart Tolle** describes this state as the "space of no-mind," where we are fully aware but not identified with our thoughts. In this space, we are free to experience the richness of life without being trapped in the mind's endless cycles of worry, regret, or anticipation. This is the essence of non-thinking: to live from a place of **awareness and presence**, beyond the limitations of the thinking mind.

The Practice of Presence: Returning to the Now

One of the key principles of non-thinking is the practice of **presence**—the ability to remain fully engaged with the present moment, without being distracted by thoughts of the past or future. In today's fast-paced world, many of us find it difficult to stay present. Our minds are constantly pulled in multiple directions, whether by technology, responsibilities, or the relentless demands of modern life.

Yet, presence is where true peace resides. The mind is a time traveler, often dwelling on past regrets or future worries, but the present moment is the only place where life truly unfolds. When we practice non-thinking, we cultivate the ability to return to the present, where we can experience life as it is, free from the distortions of mental projections.

The Zen Master **Thich Nhat Hanh** once said,

"The present moment is filled with joy and happiness. If you are attentive, you will see it."

This profound statement serves as a reminder that the peace we seek is not hidden somewhere in the future, nor is it lost in the past. It is available to us here and now, in the present moment. By practicing non-thinking, we learn to access this peace by returning to the now, again and again.

Compassion and Connection: Expanding Beyond the Self

As we cultivate non-thinking and move beyond the mind's incessant focus on the self, we naturally develop a deeper sense of **compassion** and **connection** with others. When we are no longer preoccupied with our own thoughts, fears, and desires, we become more attuned to the experiences of those around us. We begin to see that suffering is not unique to us; it is a shared aspect of the human experience. This realization opens our hearts to others, fostering a sense of empathy and compassion that transcends the ego's concerns.

Non-thinking helps us dissolve the barriers that the mind creates between "self" and "other." In the space of non-thinking, we recognize that the distinctions we make between ourselves and others are largely mental constructs, and that at a deeper level, we are all interconnected. This awareness brings with it a profound sense of unity and oneness, allowing us to engage with others from a place of genuine compassion and understanding.

In the words of **Ram Dass**,

"We're all just walking each other home."

This quote beautifully captures the essence of compassion that arises from non-thinking. When we move beyond the mind's focus on individual identity, we see that we are all part of a greater whole, and that our shared journey through life is one of mutual support and understanding.

The Journey Continues: A Lifelong Practice

While non-thinking offers a powerful path to inner peace, it is not a destination to be reached but a **lifelong practice** to be cultivated. Like any skill, it requires patience, persistence, and dedication. There will be moments when the mind's chatter seems overwhelming, when it feels impossible to step back from thoughts and simply be present. But with continued practice, the benefits of non-thinking become more apparent, and the moments of stillness and peace grow more frequent.

It is important to remember that non-thinking is not about perfection. There will be times when the mind takes over, when worries and fears arise, and when it feels difficult to find peace. These moments are not failures but opportunities for growth. Each time we notice the mind's chatter and gently return to the present, we strengthen our ability to live beyond the mind's constraints.

As the poet **Rainer Maria Rilke** once wrote,

"Be patient toward all that is unsolved in your heart
and try to love the questions themselves."

This quote reminds us that the journey of non-thinking is not about finding all the answers but about learning to live with the questions. It is about embracing the uncertainties of life with grace, trusting that peace can be found in the space of not knowing.

Beyond the Mind: A New Way of Living

In conclusion, the practice of non-thinking offers us a way to transcend the limitations of the mind and access a deeper state of **inner peace**. By detaching from the mental narratives that create suffering, we free ourselves to live more fully in the present moment, experiencing life with clarity, compassion, and joy.

Living beyond the mind is not about abandoning thought altogether, but about learning to see thoughts for what they are—temporary, fleeting, and often disconnected from reality. When we stop identifying with our thoughts, we discover a new way of living, one that is rooted in presence, awareness, and inner freedom.

As we continue on this journey of non-thinking, we begin to realize that peace is not something to be attained or achieved. It is already within us, waiting to be uncovered. The mind, with all its judgments and stories, is simply the veil that obscures this peace. By moving beyond the mind, we lift this veil and step into a state of being where suffering dissolves, and only peace remains.

In the end, non-thinking is not just a practice—it is a way of living, a way of seeing, and a way of being that allows us to experience the world as it truly is: perfect in its imperfection, dynamic in its stillness, and boundless in its potential. This shift in perspective is not a dramatic event but a gradual unfolding, a peeling away of the layers of mental noise that obscure the deep, quiet truth within each of us: that peace is our natural state, and it is accessible in every moment, once we learn to stop searching for it in the wrong places.

Living Beyond the Mind: A New Paradigm for Everyday Life

As we move forward from this exploration into non-thinking, it is crucial to recognize that **living beyond the mind** is not just about finding peace in meditation or during moments of stillness. It is about integrating this practice into every facet of life—into our relationships, our work, our challenges, and our joys. This integration of non-thinking into daily life allows us to respond to situations from a place of wisdom and balance, rather than from the habitual reactivity of the mind.

In our relationships, for example, living beyond the mind can transform the way we interact with others. Instead of allowing the mind's judgments, assumptions, or fears to dictate how we communicate, we can learn to listen more deeply, with presence and compassion. We can let go of the need to control the outcome of a conversation or to be right, and instead, approach each interaction with openness and curiosity. This shift fosters deeper connections and reduces the conflicts that often arise from misunderstandings rooted in mental projections.

Similarly, in our work and daily tasks, non-thinking helps us move beyond the stress and pressure that the mind often creates. The mind tends to frame work in terms of deadlines, performance, and success or failure. While these considerations are important, they can easily dominate our experience and lead to burnout or dissatisfaction. By cultivating non-thinking, we can approach our work with greater ease, trusting that clarity and creativity will arise naturally when we are fully present, rather than overthinking every step.

Facing Challenges with Non-Thinking: The Power of Presence in Difficulty

One of the greatest benefits of non-thinking is its ability to help us navigate life's inevitable challenges with more grace and resilience. Whether we are facing personal loss, professional setbacks, or health issues, the mind often amplifies the difficulty of these experiences by layering them with fear, anxiety, and worst-case scenarios. Non-thinking teaches us to face challenges **without adding unnecessary mental suffering** to the situation.

This does not mean that we ignore or suppress difficult emotions. On the contrary, non-thinking allows us to fully feel and process these emotions without becoming consumed by the mind's narratives about them. We learn to observe our emotions as they arise, without immediately reacting or trying to escape them. This ability to **be with what is**, even when it is uncomfortable, is one of the most powerful aspects of non-thinking.

In times of difficulty, the mind often fixates on the desire for things to be different than they are. We wish for the past to change or for the future to bring relief. But this resistance to the present moment only deepens our suffering. Non-thinking helps us release this resistance by reminding us that peace is not dependent on external circumstances—it is something we can access even in the midst of pain or uncertainty.

The spiritual teacher **Pema Chödrön** beautifully captures this idea when she says,

"You are the sky. Everything else—it's just the weather."

This quote reminds us that no matter what storms we face in life, there is a part of us—the part that resides beyond the mind—that remains untouched, clear, and at peace. By connecting with this deeper part of ourselves through non-thinking, we can weather any storm with grace and equanimity.

The Endless Journey: Cultivating Non-Thinking as a Lifelong Practice

As we have discussed, non-thinking is not a one-time achievement or a goal to be reached. It is a **lifelong practice**, one that deepens over time as we become more attuned to the subtle workings of the mind and the quiet presence that lies beyond it. There will be moments when the mind pulls us back into its familiar patterns of worry, judgment, or fear, and in those moments, it can be easy to forget the peace that non-thinking offers. But each time we notice the mind's chatter and gently return to the present moment, we strengthen our ability to live beyond the mind.

The practice of non-thinking requires patience, kindness, and a willingness to embrace imperfection. There is no need to rush or force progress. Instead, we can approach this journey with a sense of curiosity and openness, trusting that each moment of presence, no matter how fleeting, contributes to our overall growth.

It is helpful to remember that even the most experienced practitioners of mindfulness and non-thinking experience moments of mental distraction or emotional turbulence. What sets them apart is not that they never think or feel negative emotions, but that they have developed the ability to **return to presence** again and again, without judgment or frustration. This ability to gently guide ourselves back to the present is the key to making non-thinking a sustainable, lifelong practice.

Beyond the Mind: Expanding Our Understanding of Peace

As we continue on the path of non-thinking, we begin to realize that **peace is not a static state**. It is not something we achieve once and then hold onto forever. Instead, peace is dynamic, fluid, and ever-present. It is something we can tap into at any moment, regardless of what is happening in our external lives.

This understanding of peace as something that exists **beyond the mind** is transformative because it frees us from the belief that peace can only be found when our circumstances are perfect. We begin to see that peace is available to us even in the midst of chaos, conflict, or uncertainty. The mind may continue to generate thoughts, but we no longer identify with those thoughts. Instead, we rest in the awareness that lies beneath them, the awareness that is always calm, clear, and at peace.

In this way, non-thinking helps us expand our understanding of peace from something conditional and temporary to something **unconditional and enduring**. Peace is not dependent on external circumstances; it is a reflection of our ability to live beyond the mind's limited perspective.

A New Relationship with the Mind: From Master to Servant

One of the most profound shifts that non-thinking offers is the opportunity to transform our relationship with the mind. For much of our lives, we have allowed the mind to be the master, dictating our actions, decisions, and emotional responses. But through non-thinking, we learn that the mind is not meant to be the master; it is meant to be a **servant**—a powerful tool that we can use when needed but that does not control our experience of life.

When the mind becomes our servant rather than our master, we are free to use its incredible capabilities—reason, analysis, problem-solving—without being enslaved by its constant need for control. We can think when necessary and then return to presence when thinking is no longer required. This balance allows us to engage with the world more effectively while remaining grounded in inner peace.

The great philosopher **Jiddu Krishnamurti** once said,

"It is no measure of health to be well adjusted to a profoundly sick society."

This quote reminds us that the mind's relentless pursuit of control, success, and validation is not a sign of health but a symptom of a society that values doing over being, thinking over presence. Non-thinking offers us a way to break free from this conditioning and return to a more natural, balanced way of living—one that honors both the mind's capabilities and the deeper wisdom of presence.

The Ripple Effect: How Non-Thinking Impacts the World Around Us

While non-thinking is an internal practice, its effects ripple outward, impacting not only our own lives but also the lives of those around us. As we become more present, peaceful, and compassionate, we naturally begin to **influence the world in positive ways**. Our relationships become more harmonious, our interactions more genuine, and our contributions more aligned with the greater good.

In a world that is often characterized by division, conflict, and stress, the practice of non-thinking offers a path to **healing and connection**. When we live beyond the mind, we are no longer driven by the ego's need to compete, compare, or dominate. Instead, we approach others from a place of empathy and understanding, recognizing that we are all part of the same human experience.

This shift in consciousness can have a profound impact on the world. As more individuals begin to cultivate non-thinking and embrace inner peace, the collective consciousness of humanity can begin to shift as well. We move from a society based on fear, scarcity, and separation to one rooted in compassion, abundance, and unity.

A Final Thought: Beyond the Mind, Toward True Peace

In closing, the journey of non-thinking is one of the most profound and transformative paths we can take in life. It is a journey that leads us beyond the mind's limitations and into a state of **inner peace**, where suffering no longer holds sway. Through the practice of non-thinking, we learn to navigate life with greater clarity, compassion, and ease, trusting in the flow of each moment rather than clinging to the mind's need for control.

As we move beyond the mind, we discover a deeper truth: that peace is not something we need to chase or achieve; it is already within us, waiting to be uncovered. The mind, with all its thoughts, fears, and desires, is simply the surface layer. Beneath it lies a vast expanse of stillness and serenity—a place where suffering dissolves and only peace remains.

To quote the Zen Master **Shunryu Suzuki,**

"The most important thing is to find out what is the most important thing."

As we conclude this exploration of non-thinking, let this be our guiding question. What is the most important thing in your life? If it is peace, then the path forward is clear: learn to live beyond the mind, and you will discover that the peace you seek has always been with you, waiting patiently for you to return to it.

The journey continues, and each moment is an opportunity to step beyond the mind and into the present, where true peace resides. Let us walk this path with presence, with grace, and with the quiet understanding that beyond the mind lies the end of suffering and the beginning of a life lived in peace.

ABOUT THE AUTHOR

Nancy B. Blevins

Nancy B. Blevins is an author, mindfulness advocate, and teacher with a passion for helping individuals unlock the transformative power of presence and non-thinking in their everyday lives. With a background in both philosophy and psychology, Nancy has spent years studying ancient wisdom traditions, including Zen Buddhism, Taoism, and modern mindfulness practices, which all converge in her writing and teaching. Her work focuses on the intersection of mental clarity, emotional balance, and spiritual fulfillment, offering practical tools to navigate life with greater peace, purpose, and presence.

Through her writing, Nancy inspires readers to explore the depths of their minds, let go of mental patterns that create suffering, and cultivate a deeper connection to themselves and the world around them. Her unique approach blends timeless wisdom with modern insights, making her work accessible to anyone seeking inner peace and clarity in today's fast-paced, often overwhelming world.

Nancy's books are grounded in the belief that true transformation begins from within, and she is dedicated to guiding readers toward a life of mindfulness, compassion, and conscious living. When she's not writing, Nancy enjoys spending time in nature, practicing meditation, and sharing her insights through workshops and retreats.

With a commitment to fostering inner growth and resilience, Nancy B. Blevins continues to inspire countless individuals on their journey toward self-discovery and lasting peace.

Made in United States
Troutdale, OR
02/21/2025